Cambridge Studies in Social Anthropology

General Editor: Jack Goody

68

TRADITION AS TRUTH AND COMMUNICATION

A list of books in the series will be found at the end of the volume

Tradition as Truth and Communication

A cognitive description of traditional discourse

PASCAL BOYER
Fellow of King's College, Cambridge

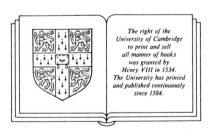

The right of the
University of Cambridge
to print and sell
all manner of books
was granted by
Henry VIII in 1534.
The University has printed
and published continuously
since 1584.

CAMBRIDGE UNIVERSITY PRESS

Cambridge
New York   Port Chester
Melbourne   Sydney

Published by the Press Syndicate of the University of Cambridge
The Pitt Building, Trumpington Street, Cambridge CB2 1RP
40 West 20th Street, New York NY 10011 USA
10 Stamford Road, Oakleigh, Melbourne 3166, Australia

© Cambridge University Press 1990

First published 1990

Printed in Great Britain by the University Press, Cambridge

British Library cataloguing in publication data

Boyer, Pascal
Tradition as truth and communication: a cognitive description of traditional discourse.
1. Society. Role of customs
I. Title
303.3′72

Library of Congress cataloguing in publication data

Boyer, Pascal
Tradition as truth and communication: a cognitive description of
traditional discourse / Pascal Boyer.
    p.   cm. — (Cambridge studies in social anthropology. 68)
Bibliography
Includes index.
ISBN 0-521-37417-0
1. Intercultural communication.   2. Cognition and culture.
3. Language and culture.   I. Title.   II. Series.
GN345.6.869   1990
303.48 2 – dc20   89-7285 CIP

ISBN 0 521 37417 0

CUP

Contents

v

Preface

Although the bulk of anthropological literature is about traditions and traditional societies, there is no such thing as a *theory* of tradition in social anthropology. As Shils puts it (1981: vii), a book about tradition is very much in need of a tradition. That anthropologists do not generally recognise the need to develop such a theory is in itself a puzzling feature of the discipline. Social or cultural anthropology began as an attempt to describe and understand exotic societies, almost all of which were traditional; the main theoretical constructions were erected to explain typically traditional ways of thinking and behaving. The functional interpretation of myth and ritual and the description of marriage prescriptions as structured exchange were meant to shed light on mainly if not exclusively traditional customs. Trobriand, Zande, Nuer and Navajo, these names used as landmarks in almost every anthropological discussion or speculation, are all names of traditional groups. When trying to uncover the whys and wherefores of strange customs, Malinowski or Evans-Pritchard certainly got the familiar, if exasperating answer 'we do that because we've always done so', 'because that's the way we do it here', 'because our fathers told us to', and so on. This does not concern the legendary pioneers only; although modern anthropology is not ill at ease in modern urban environments, it still is much more geared to describing and explaining traditional ways.

Not the problem

In the anthropological literature the characterisation of tradition is generally considered both self-evident (everyone knows what a tradition is) and immaterial (the way you understand it has no empirical consequences). Here I shall try to show that, on the contrary, it has both difficulties and consequences. One of my aims is to show that there *is* a problem, that the repetition or reiteration of tradition implies complex processes of acquisition, memorisation and social interaction which must be described and explained.

Like most anthropological categories, 'tradition' is not a proper theoretical concept. Diverse institutions are lumped together under the label

vii

'traditional', mainly on the basis of their resemblance to certain prototypical cases. There is no *a priori* reason to think that the institutions thus labelled have any scientifically relevant properties in common, in the same way as there is no reason to think that the ordinary distinction of trees and shrubs is relevant to biology; scientific categories often cut across common sense taxonomies. In other words, a theory of traditions like the one outlined here may not be a theory about all the things usually called 'traditional'. This is just because ordinary language, including its anthropological variety, is sloppy, and we must try not to be. According to Shils (1981: 12), the ordinary concept of tradition 'includes all that a society of a given time possesses and which already existed when its present possessors came upon it'. Surely, if *that* is tradition, then there cannot be a scientific theory of tradition, just as there cannot be a theory of rectangular objects or a theory of white animals. There is no reason why all the objects included should share properties other than the trivial. Understood in that way, the category is useless (as Shils himself, I hasten to add, makes clear in his book).

It is therefore important to make clear what this book is *not* about. It is not about written traditions, i.e., the conservation, transmission and exegesis of written texts or 'scriptures'. The argument here is based on examples of purely oral communication; although the interaction described can be found also in literate societies, as I will explain, it is found there in the form of an oral interaction. The question, whether the institutions described here and the conservation of texts have anything in common, is an empirical one, which surely cannot be solved unless we have a reliable description of what happens in both domains; but we have no such description so far.

Even granted this restriction, there are still many things called 'traditional' which I will not examine. Indeed, I will focus on a very narrowly defined set of institutions, in which important truths are supposed to be expressed by licenced speakers, and attention-demanding ritual gestures are performed by specific actors, all this being accomplished with reference to previous occurrences of the same statements and the same gestures. My assumption is that such situations of social interaction share certain important properties and therefore constitute a proper scientific object.

'Tradition' and psychology

Without opening a long methodological digression, I must mention the few commonsense principles I have followed here. A fundamental one is that there is no theory of what happens in cultural interaction without some strong hypotheses about what is happening in the actors' minds. So we should try to make these hypotheses explicit; if they are not plausible, we should change them so that the anthropological theories are at least compatible, if not altogether congruent, with what psychologists know about mental processes.

There are two possible ways of making psychological claims in anthropological theory. One is to make use of some precise hypotheses in experimental psychology, to examine their relevance as concerns the specific anthropological data and to put forward new explicit hypotheses where needed. From the days of Bartlett and Rivers to modern cognitive anthropology, many anthropologists have followed this path. Nothing of the kind, however, has been done about the psychology of tradition, which has been approached in the other possible manner, i.e., by considering human cognition as a 'black box' in anthropological theories. The main idea in the black box approach is that it is possible to make strong claims about the result of cognitive processes without bothering to examine how actual psychological mechanisms could bring about such phenomena. In this view, the technicalities of cognition, the workings of the black box, do not really matter; what counts is the alleged result, namely the 'conservation' of certain concepts and beliefs. When a certain property of traditions is observed, or indeed conjectured, a psychological mechanism is postulated, whose operation would give precisely such results.

Against this *ad hoc* approach, it is in fact possible to make precise claims about the processes involved in traditional interaction, and to compare them to some important findings and hypotheses of cognitive psychology. This research programme obviously implies a great deal of speculation, especially because cognitive anthropology has only recently begun to consider the domain of 'symbolism' and other such complex phenomena of interaction. However tentative and limited, the findings of cognitive psychology allow us to see why some anthropological theories are just psychologically implausible. It is often possible to replace unnecessarily complicated models with simpler psychological hypotheses. Throughout the book, I will use psychological findings in this way, as a safeguard against the multiplication of *ad hoc* entities and processes. This way of proceeding is founded on two assumptions which, I suppose, do not need to be justified in great detail: one is that unnecessary entities should not be multiplied; the other is that one should not place too much confidence in anthropological analytical concepts. Most of them are more like 'phlogiston' than 'oxygen'; they do not refer to real things in the world, and they designate problems instead of solving them. This is why I have dispensed, as much as possible, with such terms as 'symbols', 'cultural models' or 'socialisation'. Important (and unsolved) problems are often concealed under these familiar categories.

Lastly, I must point out that the ethnographic examples given in support of various hypotheses must be treated in the same way as examples in all anthropological theories, i.e., as suggestive illustrations rather than definitive proofs. Most of the recurrent patte.ns the theory is based on are well known to anthropologists. This is why the analysis of all the implications of theory, at each step of the argument, is given priority over the elaboration of suggestive ethnographic descriptions. As a consequence, what is proposed at the end of the book is a set of general *hypotheses*, which further empirical material should flesh out, modify and possibly refute.

Acknowledgements

The ideas developed here are the distant outcome of long conversations with Anne de Sales and Michael Houseman about possible formal theories of the 'cultural world'. Notes and references cannot do justice to the inspiration drawn from constant interaction with them, and with Carlo Severi who provided so many inspiring ideas and criticisms. I would not have developed and corrected the original draft without the substantial help and stimulating environment provided by the University of Cambridge. I am especially grateful to Jack Goody for inviting me over and helping me in so many ways. St John's College and King's College gave me the means to do the research and discuss its results. I also benefited from the detailed comments and criticisms on a first version of this book and several related papers, especially those made by Cornelia Sorabji, Nick Thomas, Tanya Luhrmann, Declan Quigley, Caroline Humphrey, Andras Zempleni, Esther Goody, Geoffrey Lloyd and Ernest Gellner.

1

Conserved world-views or salient memories?

The 'traditional' cultural phenomena concerned here can be briefly characterised by the following features:

(i) they are *instances of social interaction*:
(ii) they are *repeated*;
(iii) they are *psychologically salient*.

Let me comment briefly on these abstract phrases, using a prototypical case of the sort of institutions I will talk about. After his first trance, a newly initiated shaman tells an audience of fellow-shamans and villagers of the contract he has made with the spirits of the jungle. I will call this event 'traditional'. This usage of the term is not really contentious. It is important, however, to be clear about what sort of objects we are dealing with; otherwise some crucial (and typical) mistakes may creep in and make the discussion hopelessly confused.

First, what I mean by saying that I will deal with instances of social interaction is simply that we are concerned here with *actual events*, with the things people actually do and ethnographers observe, not the things anthropologists think should be posited in order to explain what people do. That is to say, the social phenomenon considered here, and labelled 'traditional' is the shaman's singing, more precisely the social event of the shaman's singing to a certain type of audience, about a certain type of mystical experience, etc. Now an anthropological account of this event should include many other things, notably a series of hypotheses about the organisation of people's ideas, the social organisation of the place, people's emotional involvement in the ritual, and so on. In the anthropological usage, both these underlying things and the social events are called 'traditional'. This confusion, as we will see, is the root of some very problematic claims about tradition. In order to avoid conceptual promiscuity, we should therefore try and keep separate labels for the phenomena we observe and the underlying processes we hypothesise. Here the *events* will be called 'traditional'. In the following pages I will try to examine general properties

1

of 'traditional contexts' and 'traditional situations'; such terms will always refer to specific social events.

Let me now turn to a more difficult point. The events described here as 'traditional' are *repeated* events. It is important to understand that this is a criterion of recognition, not a theoretical claim, in the same way as telling someone that 'giraffes' are 'these tall animals with a very long neck' gives them a criterion to identify what is being referred to, nothing more. So we will call the event of the shaman's singing 'traditional' because it is a repeated event, because it is performed with reference to previous occurrences of the same type of social event. This, in practice, is how anthropologists recognise that they are dealing with a traditional institution: at people's constant reference to past occurrences, and at the resemblance between these occurrences. Not to put too fine a point on it, repetition is an observational term.

It is very difficult, however, not to make a fatal mistake here, which consists in equating the repetition of occurrences and the conservation of a model. The event of the shaman's singing seems very similar to what happened when other shamans were initiated, two years ago, ten years ago, and so on. It seems reasonable to surmise that there is some cultural model of 'shamanistic initiation singing', which seems to be conserved over the years. Indeed, it may be the most reasonable hypothesis, but we must remain aware of the fact that this 'conservation' is not an observed property of the events, but a hypothesis put forward in order to account for their actual repetition. This distinction, however pedestrian, is crucial because if the 'conservation of models' is a hypothesis, then it may be false and it must be discussed. One just cannot take it for granted; supporting evidence is required.[1]

We will not examine all the aspects of repeated social interaction, and that is why the third criterion is pertinent. The shaman, to return to our example, probably uses a language whose vocabulary, syntax and phonology are very much the same as thirty years before. That is not what we want to explain. On the other hand, anthropologists are interested in explaining why these initiation journeys should be sung rather than talked about, why it is deemed necessary to induce a trance, or why the whole process is supposed to cure someone's disease. To borrow a term from G. Lewis's study of ritual (1980), we are interested in the 'attention-demanding' aspects of these institutions. An utterance of a gesture will not be considered traditional if it does not focalise people's attention more than ordinary discourse or actions. Psychological salience, therefore, is another criterion of recognition.

Again, these criteria do not constitute a 'definition' of tradition. They are simply used here in order to pick out a certain class of social phenomena; although they are no doubt too vague, I hope they make it possible to *recognise* the class of institutions the argument will be about. In fact, recognition should not be too difficult, since such institutions (myth, 'religious' or 'political' ritual, etc.), are the subject-matter of most classical anthropological monographs and theories so far. Whether it is legitimate to give the term 'tradition' this narrow extension is a purely terminological question. As long as the reference is recognised, my 'traditional' institutions could as well be called 'XYZ'; but that would be just too awkward.

The point of a theory of 'tradition' (as identified here, henceforth without quotes) is to describe the general processes whereby the salient aspects of certain phenomena of social interaction are repeated or reiterated. There is no satisfactory anthropological theory to deal with this problem. The aim of this chapter is to show that the anthropological answers are unsatisfactory, not only because the solutions are empirically wrong, but also because the problem itself has been misconstrued. In order to go further, we must therefore examine and discuss some common assumptions about traditional actions and utterances. Unfortunately, the 'common' conception, precisely because it is common, is almost always left implicit. It is not explained in theoretical essays or general textbooks, but it is pervasive in ethnographic descriptions and the generalisations based on them. So it takes a little reading between the lines to uncover and discuss it. I must admit right now that my description of common anthropological views is intended as a springboard for further speculation rather than a detailed analysis of the discipline's implicit premises.

The 'common' conception of tradition

When doing fieldwork in a traditional environment, an anthropologist is bound to give some kind of answer to the question, why and how the institutions identified as traditional get repeated. And the type of answer he or she gives to that question reflects in the particular hypotheses put forward about those specific institutions. Things are not so simple, however, and the question of repetition is almost always coupled with another one, which concerns the 'cohesiveness' of the institutions considered, i.e., what keeps them together; to put it in a less abstract way, what is the link between, e.g., the specific initiation song for shamans, people's utterances about spirits and the fact that shamans are said by an informant to cure other people? There is no *a priori* reason why the questions of repetition and cohesiveness should be examined together; as we will see, however, the 'common' anthropological treatment of repetition implies a strong hypothesis about cohesiveness, and *vice versa*.

The question of cohesiveness is answered in a way which reflects pervasive anthropological assumptions about culture and society in general. The idea is that utterances, actions and more generally the bits and pieces of behaviour anthropologists observe and record, are in fact held together by some

3

underlying intellectual objects. These are called 'world-views', 'cultural models', 'local theories', 'collective representations', etc. There is a considerable ambiguity in anthropological literature about: (i) what part of these objects is supposed to be in people's minds and what part is the combination of what different actors know and think; (ii) how implicit or unconscious they are; and (iii) to what extent they are a reality or a model of it.[2] Here I will not examine these ideas at such an abstract level. I will only discuss their consequences as regards the treatment of traditional institutions. The main point of this conception is that traditionl phenomena are linked to, and explained by a set of underlying ideas or representations.

As for the question of traditionality, the common answer is that some groups and societies are 'conservative' or 'traditionalistic'; they are so organised that change is ruled out or deemed dangerous or interpreted as a threat to the social order. This is construed as a characteristic either of the social groups, the organisation of which inevitably favours the reproduction of past practice, or of the people, who are naturally conservative or frightened for some reason at the possibility of change. And it is often assumed that this in fact is the normal or natural state of affairs in human societies; the problem then is to understand how some societies, like modern Western ones, seem to foster the idea that change is welcome or inevitable.

These assumptions are generally supposed to be unproblematic. They are seldom discussed, or even presented in too much detail. Anthropology textbooks for example generally gloss over the exact status of collective representations, or present a few examples of traditional 'conservatism', to give readers the feel of the thing. Anthropological assumptions are thus taken as a matter of fact, rather than as hypotheses which could be discussed in terms of plausibility and heuristic value. To cite but one example, in a rigorous and detailed study of anthropological theories of religion, J. Skorupski has no compunction in writing that a traditional believer sticks to his creed 'precisely because he is traditionalistic' (1976: 204). That an otherwise punctilious author should not mind the tautology is an indication of how natural and self-evident the idea of 'conservatism' or 'traditionalism' is supposed to be. It is no surprise, then, that these ideas are in most cases left implicit. This makes our discussion much more difficult, as we always run the risk of creating the easy target of an anthropological strawman. It may be of help here to consider one of the very few explicit conceptions of tradition, that put forward by R. Horton in a series of papers on the comparison of African traditional thought and Western science (1967a and b, 1970, 1982).

According to Horton, traditional thought as a whole should be considered as an attempt to reach a *theoretical* understanding of the world, essentially comparable to scientific theorising. Theories are built in order to explain events by integrating them into 'a wider causal context'. In traditional

4

thought as in Western modernity, according to Horton, we can find two levels of thinking and discourses: that of 'primary theory' (i.e., common sense or everyday notions about the world) and that of 'secondary theory' (tradition in one case, science in the other) which is supposed to make up for the 'incompetence' of everyday knowledge in certain areas of human experience (1982: 229). Primary theory is built on common sense forms of reasoning which seem to be much the same in all societies; its explanations resort to a 'push-pull' type of causality, linking observable events which concern middle- sized objects. On the contrary, secondary theory resorts to 'hidden entities' (like waves and particles in Western physics, deities and mystical substances in traditional thought). Horton then proceeds to the distinction between traditional secondary theories and modern scientific ones; two features can serve as fundamental criteria of demarcation. Traditional theories are founded upon a 'traditionalistic' view of knowledge, i.e., the assumption that knowledge handed down from former generations is necessarily better than new adaptations, because it is 'time-tested' (1982: 238). Also, tradition resorts to a 'consensual mode of theorising', 'in which all members of a community...share a single over-arching framework of secondary-theoretical assumptions and carry out intellectual innovation within that framework' (1982: 229). Alternative theories generate anxiety because they break this social consensus. On the contrary, Western scientific thought is anti-traditionalistic (more recent theories are supposed to be better) and resorts to a competitive mode of theorising.[3]

Obviously, we are dealing here with a particularly strong formulation of the common assumptions. Horton is not satisfied with such vague anthropological constructs as 'world-views' and 'conceptions'; for him, traditional phenomena are the expression of *theories*. It is clear in his first papers that the term must be taken in a strong sense; traditional thought, just as modern scientific theorising, produces sets of beliefs that are (i) integrated (ii) consistent and (iii) explanatory. Anthropologists however are constantly dealing with utterances and actions that seem inconsistent or paradoxical, and usually demand more explanation and interpretation than they provide. So they cannot be entirely at ease with Horton's strong claims. Hence a long and heated controversy about the *format* of the 'theories' anthropologists are expected to find underlying traditional phenomena.[4] Here I will not dwell on the intricacies of that discussion, most participants of which shared what I called the 'common assumptions' about tradition, namely (i) that traditions are conserved because people want to transmit them unchanged, and (ii) that they are held together by some underlying ideas which constitute a general description of the world. These are the hypotheses I will challenge, and I think my arguments apply to all versions of these ideas, from Horton's very strong formulation to the 'soft', watered down version that can be found in other authors.

5

In the rest of this chapter I will try to show that such an approach replaces a genuine empirical question, about the processes of repetition, with question-begging abstract explanations. To return to the example mentioned at the beginning, we want to account for the repetition of a certain type of social interaction, e.g., between a newly initiated shaman, his colleagues, an ill person and an audience; we want to know why all this is attention-demanding; we want to explain why only certain aspects of the interaction are reproduced, while others are forgotten or left aside. These are difficult empirical questions, and the search for general properties of such interactions demands a painstaking process of hypothesis building and testing. If, on the other hand, we just assume that all this happens because people 'stick to their traditional theories', the whole question is magically eliminated. The 'solution', however, does not really hold; in order to see how much it is on the wrong track, however, and to grasp exactly what is wrong with this pervasive conception of traditions, it may be of help to present a more detailed ethnographic example.

Fang literary tradition

The example is that of a traditional literature I have observed and studied, that of the Fang of Gabon, Cameroon and Equatorial Guinea.[5] The main genre is called *mvet*, after the name of the harp which is used to accompany the singers. The repertoire is composed of extremely long and complex epic stories, most of which narrate the interminable wars between two clans of mythic heroes, the immortal giants of the village Engong and the mortal lineage of Oku, who try to steal their secret 'life medicine', the secret of immortality. Numerous characters are involved in the intricate plots; most of them are fierce heroes who straddle giant iron elephants and throw rainbows or red-hot iron balls at each other; in case of danger they often make a quick escape beneath the earth or above the sky. They slay each other by the thousand, and cases of magic resuscitation are not uncommon.

The mvet stories are told only by specialised singers, who have undergone a long and difficult personal initiation under some reputed poet's supervision. Becoming a singer is very much conceived of as the equivalent of becoming a witch-doctor. The rituals are quite similar, as well as the ambiguous reputation. Both initiations enable one to master the domain of witchcraft, due to a special relationship with the ancestors; but this capacity may also be used for other, anti-social purposes, so that most villagers are rather leery of these uncanny practitioners. A mvet session is an important social event; people from neighbouring villages gather at night in a 'men's house' and the session usually lasts until dawn. The epic is interwoven with other literary pieces, notably an obscure account of the singer's own initiation, together with anecdotes, jokes, proverbs, etc. Mvet story-telling appears to be one of

6

the main elements of Fang tradition. In those sessions, it is generally agreed, important truths about such matters as ancestors or witchcraft are communicated; these important ideas cannot be reached in ordinary contexts. Mvet players are among the initiates, those who know about past knowledge and hidden entities. Moreover, mvet-related knowledge is all the more valued as it is a marker of identity. Although neighbouring groups have equivalent and often very similar genres, mvet is considered as exclusively Fang.

The storytelling sessions have all the usual characteristics of a traditional phenomenon. They are performed by authoritative specialists who constantly refer to knowledge transmitted across generations, during long initiation rituals. The picture is, however, more ambiguous if we try to *describe* the 'world-view' or 'conceptions' expressed. One of the striking features of the mvet stories is that most crucial notions in Fang discourse are used here in a puzzling way, often contradictory or paradoxical. A revealing example is the way the ancestors are described; they are mentioned in both the stories and the narrative of the singer's initiation. Both descriptions are quite complicated; the ancestors' unpredictable behaviour brings about sudden *coups de théâtre* in the narration. As for the lyrical evocation of the singer's initiation, it is generally so obscure that even the competent ancestor-cult specialists get bogged down in the intricacies of the poet's adventures. To compound these difficulties, both descriptions are strikingly different from, and sometimes incompatible with, what is received as common wisdom about ancestors. The same can be said about the other conceptual domains evoked during the mvet sessions; if epic stories and songs convey a world-view, it certainly gets very muddled in the process. This does not mean that some kind of conception is not expressed, but that it is certainly difficult for the audience to represent what it consists of.

In such a context, the idea that some 'world-view' is conserved across generations is rather difficult to evaluate. The first good texts were recorded in 1959 (see Zwè Nguéma 1972) and a comparison with epics recorded in 1981, from the next generation of singers, shows little change insofar as the style, characters and main plots are concerned. This, however, concerns the 'surface' of the institution; it would be wrong to infer that any important 'meanings' have been conserved, since it is quite difficult to describe them at any stage of the institution.

The problems described here are not specific to Fang literature; most anthropologists have that kind of difficulty when trying to identify or describe the 'conceptions' behind instances of traditional interaction. African traditional literature and Amerindian shamanism elude such descriptions in the same way. These difficulties, however, are not only the result of incomplete ethnographic descriptions. They indicate a more fundamental problem, concerning the lack of 'fit' between the cultural phenomena

7

observed and the predictions of the theory. In the rest of this chapter I will expand on this point, and try to re-formulate the problem in a way that is more consistent with the type of data anthropologists actually gather.

Digression: is long-term conservation relevant?

Before proceeding to the discussion of the common paradigm, however, the Fang example will allow me to introduce an important distinction, between the phenomena a theory of traditions is supposed to explain and those outside its scope. In the above description I have left aside what some anthropologists may consider the crucial problem about traditional situations: is the alleged 'conservation' of cultural material *real*? that is, do groups or people involved in traditional interaction really conserve the same form of interaction over generations? In the 'common' conception described above, the question is either avoided or treated in a rather agnostic way. People stick to established 'conceptions' or 'world-views'; what matters is that they *believe* those conceptions to be 'time-tested', not that they are actually conserved over long periods. A striking illustration of this pervasive view is that, although most anthropologists focus on traditional interaction, they seldom study it across time, measuring its changes over long periods; and those who do are led to emphasise change rather than permanence. So is the permanence of tradition anything but an illusion? In the course of trying to describe traditions as empirical phenomena, I have found, to my own surprise, that this in fact is one of the least important and difficult questions posed by traditions. Without anticipating too much on the rest of the argument, I must indicate briefly why the questions of stability and change will not be discussed at much length here.

What is described as traditional in ethnography consists of actions or utterances which are performed with the guidelines provided by people's memories of a previous occurrence. For instance, this year's fertility rites are performed in a certain way because that is the way the specialists and other participants remember the other years' festivals. In the long run, this process may well result in a gradual and thorough change; it may also result in near perfect repetition. Now whether things go one way or the other depends on historical and ecological factors which are largely independent of the fact that the ritual is traditional.

Let me return to the example of Fang epic poetry. It is traditional in the sense that the essential features of the communicative event are repeated, and that people's memories of previous sessions provide the standard against which present performance is evaluated. The complex apprenticeship followed by young men until they become fully fledged epic poets is largely based on the memorisation of whole stories and should normally result in the reproduction of themes and style from generation to generation. Storytelling sessions however do not happen in a cultural or historical vacuum; the relevance of the epic motifs depends on what representations the audience can associate with them or infer from them. When G. Tessmann, the first reliable ethnographer in the area, transcribed fragments of epic songs in 1913, these could be considered as 'war-songs'. Violent inter-clan and inter-ethnic feuds were rife at the time, and epic poetry was meant to inspire bellicose enthusiasm. Two generations later, however, the colonial and post-colonial national order has put an end to traditional warfare. Epic combats are more obviously 'mythical' than in Tessmann's time. The evocation of witchcraft powers, on the other hand, is certainly more central than it used to be, as the colonial order is widely interpreted as a period of thriving sorcery. Now the fact that story-telling has changed in content and relevance does not mean that it is not traditional; conversely, the fact that it is traditional does not imply that it conveys the same representations and has the same effect on successive generations.[6]

The phenomenon a theory of tradition must explain is why and how it seems so natural to people, in certain circumstances, to take last year's or last decade's version of some myth or ritual as the only relevant way of performing these actions. This, as we will see, is an important empirical question, which cannot be solved in the usual, question-begging way or with tautological hypotheses. The theory therefore focuses on the *process* of traditional repetition, and must leave aside the question whether the process leads to actual cultural permanence across many generations, because this result is only partly dependent upon the process. To take a distant analogy, a good theory of reproduction should explain the processes whereby living beings generate other living beings which are very similar to them. One cannot expect the theory to explain the evolution of species, because such factors as mutation and adaptation are outside its scope.[7]

The reason why these questions are confused is that anthropology once believed it could kill two birds with one stone, as it were, namely explain both traditional repetition and the historical evolution of societies within the same theory. This led to the fabrication of such fictions as 'cool' or ahistorical societies, to the description of current hunting groups as similar to paleolithic ancestors, etc. Such ideas relied on two confusions: (i) between a form of interaction (tradition) and the kind of societies where this interaction seems predominant (I will return to this point in the last chapter); (ii) more importantly for our present argument, a confusion between describing a process and describing its output in all possible circumstances. The latter confusion is the one we must avoid here. What we are aiming for is a description and explanation of the processes whereby past occurrences of an interaction are the reference of present occurrences. This phenomenon is extremely widespread, it constitutes the subject matter of many anthro-pological descriptions. It has different long-term results, depending on extraneous factors; but we do not want to describe these factors here, only the process itself.

Problems generated by the common conception

We started with an empirical question; we wanted to know why and how certain salient forms of social interaction get repeated. We noticed that the anthropological ideas about tradition, however pertinent, do not address our original problem directly. Traditions as effectively studied are clusters of repeated, salient, etc., *events*. General theories of tradition, on the other hand, focus on intellectual constructions ('world-views', 'conceptions', 'models', 'theories', etc.. Instead of dealing with the repetition of actual interaction, they focus on the conservation of underlying cultural models. Obviously, this is a different question; while repeated events are observed, conserved ideas are hypothesised. The two problems just cannot be confused.

The reasons why anthropologists substitute conservation for repetition and models for actions is that they have an *implicit causal hypothesis*. Cultural models cause actual behaviour, and their conservation causes traditional repetition. People repeat rituals because rituals express ideas and people think ideas ought to be conserved. Obviously, there are many nuances and subtler formulations, but the hypothesis is there. Indeed, it has to be there, otherwise there would be no reason to describe traditional institutions in terms of underlying conceptions. The causal hypothesis is not really discussed, because it is viewed as self-evident; as a result it is not even considered a hypothesis at all, rather a fact of the matter. Now, if we take seriously the fact that it is a hypothesis, we must examine its 'cost' and compare it to rival explanations. Amazingly, these aspects are almost never envisaged in anthropological discussions, so that we have a theory of tradition without any examination of what other explanations would be like, therefore without any *argument*. Here I will first focus on the 'cost' of the hypothesis. The common anthropological claims are not as trivial and self-evident as they may seem. They are 'expensive' in two ways; first they do not fit the data very neatly, so that one has to put forward additional hypotheses, to bridge the gap, as it were. Second, they imply some strong claims about the way people's minds work when processing traditional actions and utterances. Obviously, the fact that a hypothesis is expensive does not entail that it is wrong, unless we have rival hypotheses which will do the job without the expense. I will try to show that this is precisely the case.

Let me first focus on the cost of the claims, and on the problem of 'fit' mentioned above. The traditional phenomena observed are series of repeated actions and utterances. Although it seems reasonable to suppose that there are some underlying conceptions, describing them and establishing the link between them and the 'surface' phenomena are no easy tasks. In general essays about 'tradition', the claims about cohesiveness and repetition seem simple, almost self-evident; in practice, they lead to worrying difficulties, especially if we take them for the explanation of traditional repetition. This, I will argue, is because some crucial features of the cultural phenomena at hand are neglected in the abstract description. It is important to identify these characteristics, because they may suggest another approach to traditions. By the same token, this discussion will allow me to refine the cursory description of traditional institutions given at the beginning of this chapter.

An important feature of traditional practice is that, in most cases, the actors do not bother to justify or rationalise it. Typically, the anthropologist is told 'we do this because we've always done so' or 'because it must be so, otherwise it would not be proper' or 'because the ancestors told us to do it', and this type of statement is certainly part of the specific intellectual climate of traditional institutions. This of course does not mean that traditional practice is without rhyme or reason, but, more precisely, that traditional things seem to provide their own justification. Performing a certain ritual, for instance, is of course justified in terms of practical goals: solving a conflict, healing a person or placating the ancestors. But the fact that the ritual has to be performed in a specific way, by specific people, does not seem to require any explanation; it is amply justified by the ritual itself. The mvet epics for instance could be sung at noon by uninitiated women, instead of at night by initiated men. But *that* would not be mvet, for the Fang; why is that? Because mvet is, precisely, something that is sung by initiated men at night. I do not mean to deny that in some places people are eager to explicate, justify and rationalise their traditional rituals. I am only suggesting that such explanations are not a *necessary* condition of such rituals, since (i) they are absent in many societies and (ii) when they are present, even anthropologists take them for *a posteriori* constructions rather than the *raison d'être* of ritual action.

Another important property that is often neglected or misunderstood is what I would call the *literalism* of repetition. People do not seem to consider that a description of a certain event, however faithful, can have the same cognitive effects as the original version. This is especially striking when applied to utterances; rather than explaining the point of a certain statement, people tend to repeat it literally and to avoid paraphrase and interpretations. When commenting on a statement made by a mvet singer or a witch-doctor, Fang people are careful to preserve its exact wording, even if a more colloquial or less ambiguous version is available. This is all the more striking as 'literalism' is absent from *everyday* conservations. This literal style is probably among the intuitive criteria that help anthropologists recognise a traditional institution. It is, however, very easy to muddle the issue by saying that people are 'conservative', so that they stick to the very form of the statements, and not only to their content. Again, this may be plausible, but it is an interpretation, not a fact. The point I made above, about repetition, applies here in the same way: a property of people's utterances is not the same as a common hypothesis that seems to account for it.

A related characteristic is that traditional institutions are pervaded with 'event-talk' rather than 'theory-talk'. That is to say, people seem to find the actual traditional utterances or actions more attention-demanding than a generalising commentary. Informants asked to comment on, for example, whether ancestors are jealous of living people are more willing to refer to singular situations than general principles; they will use a series of concrete examples and leave their moral implicit. Every anthropologist knows that it is usually much easier to elicit a description of a specific ritual, performed by specific persons, than an explanation of its underlying principles or general structure. This is not only an artefact of the ethnographic situation. Traditional institutions are generally 'transmitted' without explicit tuition; people may have the same ideas on ancestors as the older generation, but they did not receive these ideas in the form of generalising 'lessons'. Instead, what they received were countless examples of specific situations or specific problems. This focus on events is even clearer in cases where an initiation ritual is involved. Many forms of traditional action may be performed only by people who have undergone a specific initiation; such rituals (on which more in chapter 6) provide people with all sorts of salient memories, but they do not give much in terms of explicit principles about, e.g., ancestors, witchcraft and water-spirits.

This description is no doubt too vague and intuitive. But I hope it makes it clear that the 'common' anthropological idea of traditions as the expression of underlying conceptions is not as simple and evident as it first sounds. When applied to concrete cases of traditional practice, it generates difficult problems. When confronted with more general properties of traditions, it seems strangely inadequate. Again, this does not necessarily imply that the common assumptions are false; it just means that they cannot be taken for granted.

Things get even worse if we focus on the additional or ancillary hypotheses required, in order that the common conception can be applied. For instance, the claims are about 'conceptions' and theories, but people seem mainly to focus on events, on actual situations of traditional interaction, while general principles are difficult to elicit. A way of bridging the gap is to assume that the conceptions we are supposed to describe are implicit or unconscious. This is not necessarily an absurd hypothesis, but it generates some new problems. For one thing, it makes it difficult to maintain the second claim, namely that traditions get repeated because people are conservative. For how could people be conservative about things they are not aware of? In the same way, traditional literalism is puzzling if we stick to the idea that traditions express theories about the world. Usually, people engaged in theory-building are more interested in their theory's capacity to explain this or that event than in its exact wording. This could be solved with another ancillary hypothesis, to the effect that the distinction between the content and the formulation of a theory does not always hold; that is, some people may believe that changing the words will inevitably change the theory itself. Again, this claim does not seem too absurd, but it entails that people are aware that there *is* an underlying theory – so it cannot be unconscious after all. Why then is it so difficult to elicit? I will not try to solve these puzzles here. My aim is just to show that the common claims about traditions *are* problematic. The hypothesis, that traditional interaction can be studied as the expression of conceptions and world-views, generates all sorts of difficult problems.[8]

Repetition and conservatism: a reformed common conception

There are two possible ways of dealing with traditional repetition; it can be described either as an *intentional* process or as an *automatic* one, i.e., either as something that happens because people want it to happen, or as a process that is quite independent of people's desires. The 'common' anthropological conception, obviously, favours the intentional hypothesis; it claims that traditional interaction is repeated because people or groups are 'conservative'. This is often presented as a matter of fact, or even as a universal fact of human psychology, without much explanation. The common conception, however, would have a hard time trying to explain exactly what people are conservative *about*. The obvious choice, which would make the theory at least coherent, would be to say that they are conservative about underlying conceptions and world-views. This, as I said above, would be extremely problematic; if people are conservative about conceptions, then the conceptions must be explicitly represented; but there is good evidence that they are not. We have a set of interactions which get repeated. We also have a set of important characteristics like literalism and event-talk, which imply that people's attention is focused on what could be called 'superficial aspects' of the interaction, as opposed to their 'deep', underlying aspects.

The only alternative left is that people are conservative about these 'surface' properties they seem so much interested in. We may therefore suppose that what are transmitted are these aspects themselves, not the underlying objects one may hypothesise in order to make the actions reasonable. In other words, interaction is traditional because people repeat certain sets of actions and utterances, not because they hold the same 'theories' as former generations. This hypothesis seems overwhelmingly supported by the evidence on traditional interaction. As I said above, people involved in such interaction tend to focus on its surface aspects rather than any 'deep' properties: on the words of the songs and the gestures of the

13

ritual. People just do not transmit the meaning of a myth or a ritual. They give other people the details of the stories, and the precise recipe for performing the ritual in a proper way. They seldom comment on the theoretical principles expressed by the ritual action, they rather argue about its details. They are therefore interested in literal repetition and find modifications or paraphrases not quite proper. They tell anthropologists that it would be a very serious mistake, e.g., to say the spell four times instead of three, or to use parrots' feathers for the masks instead of cassowaries', and so on. Their 'conservatism', if there is such a thing, is directed at surface properties, not underlying constructs.

So it seems possible to interpret traditional repetition as the consequence of this 'conservatism'. The hypothesis, then, is that *the cause of traditional repetition is people's conservatism about the surface properties of interaction.* This hypothesis I will call the 'reformed' common conception. It can be found, implicitly, in many ethnographic descriptions. With the earlier version, described above, it shares the idea that traditional repetition is an intentional process, that it happens because people want it to happen. There is a crucial difference, however. If we admit the reformed conception, then we give up the idea that traditions should be described as the expression of underlying conceptions and world-views. Two important points should be mentioned here, if only to avoid premature misunderstanding.

(i) this hypothesis does not imply that 'conceptions' and the like do not exist. One can hold the hypothesis, and still believe that conceptions and world-views are legitimate objects of inquiry, in all available versions of this idea: with the intellectual objects being in the anthropologist's model or in the actors' minds, with them being unconscious or simply implicit, etc. What the hypothesis says is just that they are not the cause of traditional repetition; neither conceptions and world-views, whatever they are, nor people's attitudes to them (if they have any), suffice to produce repetition;

(ii) also, in case the terms 'deep' and 'superficial' should become confusing, the hypothesis is not based on the premise that people's representations are less 'abstract' than anthropological models. It may be tempting to consider world-views and conceptions as 'abstract' ideas, while memories of actual interaction are 'concrete'. This certainly applies to anthropological texts, where actual interaction is used as an example of the claims about cultural conceptions. But we are talking here about people's mental representations. And there is no reason to assume that memorising situations involves 'concrete' ideas, while thinking that 'spirits are mischievous' is more 'abstract', a point to which I will return in the last chapter;

(iii) obviously, saying that the cause of repetition is conservatism, i.e., a psychological attitude, does not mean that only psychological factors are involved. By dropping a lighted cigarette, one may cause a forest fire; now the fact that a fire occurs of course depends on many other factors: trees being highly flammable objects, some oxygen being available, gravity pulling the dropped cigarette to the ground instead of launching it on orbit, etc. But these facts are irrelevant; all we want to say is that, had the cigarette not been dropped, the forest would not have caught fire. The theory just claims that, were not some instances of social interaction represented in a specific way, their repetition would not occur.

The 'reformed' conception seems to win on all fronts, as it were. First, it is empirically plausible. Contrary to the idea that people stick to established 'theories', which flew in the face of the facts, the idea that they stick to established practice seems undeniable. Second, it has a simple, not too far-fetched hypothesis about traditional repetition. Third, it can even devise some hypotheses to deal with the underlying objects that fill anthropological descriptions. World-views, for instance, could be seen as the consequence of shared practice. People who learn a language with native speakers will end up sharing their syntax and morphology, even if they have never been 'taught' the grammar, and are still not aware of its structure. In much the same way, people who perform rituals together could end up having the same conceptions of spirits and ancestors, just because everyone derives these ideas from the rituals. So all the important questions seem to be solved in a satisfactory way. Are they really?

Unfortunately, the main hypothesis in the reformed conception turns out to be its Achilles' heel. It is assumed that the cause of traditional repetition is people's conservatism. To be more precise, this means that people's conservatism about some surface properties of previous occurrences (words, gestures, etc.) is the cause of their presence in subsequent occurrences of social interaction. There are two problems with this simple claim; first, it is empirically false; second, it is based on a very odd view of human cognitive processes.

The hypothesis is false: it says that what people want to remember is reproduced, and, conversely, that what is reproduced is what people wanted to remember. There are many counter-examples to both claims. First, many salient aspects of social interaction can be repeated without anyone being 'conservative' about them. Conversely, there are countless examples of people being 'conservative' about something, without succeeding in preserving it. 'Conservatism' is neither a necessary nor a sufficient condition for the preservation or repetition of salient aspects of social interaction.[9] If we want to identify the cause of traditional repetition, 'conservatism' is not a good candidate (I will return to this point presently, and try to explain why it *sounds* like a good candidate).

There is another problem with the 'reformed' conception. In the intentional conceptions, human memory is considered as a storage mechanism which is more or less under people's control. People want to store certain things, and simply do it; there does not seem to be any difficult 'technical' problem involved. All 'important' items are conserved, all the rest is discarded. This idea of human memory is psychologically implausible.[10] Yet it is pervasive in anthropology, because it seems congruent to what the actors say; in many groups where traditional institutions are socially important, accurate memorisation is praised, and having 'a good memory' is a highly valued skill. This discourse is of course founded on the idea that memory is a storage device controlled by the person. Now the fact that many people have this conception of their cognitive capacities does not imply that it is a true conception; psychology would be much easier, if everything people believed about their minds was true. An elementary fact of psychology is that most memory processes are out of the user's control; the latter's ability to modify or improve the storage capacity or fidelity only concerns a very small portion of what they actually remember. The memorisation processes involved in traditional repetition are likely to display the same aspects. Contrary to what an intentional conception must assume, there is no *direct* relationship between wanting to remember something and actually succeeding in recalling it; people are forever forgetting crucial data and remembering irrelevant material. In other words, people certainly have good *reasons* to remember certain things and forget others; unfortunately, such reasons are not always the *cause* of their remembering and forgetting.

So the 'reformed' theory cannot be true, at least in this formulation. The surface properties of interaction are repeated, and people sound conservative about these properties. It seems therefore reasonable to suppose that these aspects are repeated *because* people want them to be 'conserved'. This, in fact, is where the crucial mistake was made, and I will argue that the 'reformed' conception, together with many anthropological theories, has been led astray by its vocabulary and the implicit assumptions it carries.

People involved in some traditional interaction tend to think that all its surface properties are crucially important. So, given that previous occurrences of the interaction serve as a constant reference, they are likely to focus on exact repetition and reiteration. Now describing this as 'conservatism' or 'traditionalism' is wrong for many reasons. These are ordinary language words which carry all sorts of common beliefs, and could therefore preempt a precise description of the phenomenon at hand. This is precisely what happens here. 'Conservative' or 'traditionalistic' people, in ordinary language, want social interaction to stay the same either because they find change unbearable, or, in a slightly less crude way, because they think any partial change will contaminate the whole; see, e.g., people who want the Church to stick to its rites because otherwise everything will become an object of argument, and belief will disappear. So if one is a 'conservative', one is very likely to display some form of literalism about social interaction.

This, however, does not imply that the converse is true, that is, that a literalist behaviour necessarily implies some form of 'conservatism'. Indeed, there are many forms of literalist behaviour that have nothing to do with conservatism at all. Computer science teachers will typically insist that their students, when writing a programme, use spaces, indentations and punctuation marks in the precise manner they have been taught. Obviously, there is no conservatism here, just the (true) belief that any change of this kind will preclude successful computing. So one can be 'literalist' and insist on literal repetition because one thinks the desired effects will be brought about by the surface properties of the object. This is precisely the attitude of people involved in traditional interaction. As I mentioned above, traditional literalism means that one takes, e.g., the precise gestures of a ritual, their order, the fact that only certain persons may participate, the allocation of roles during the ceremony, as the essential aspects without which one is not performing the ritual at all. To take another example, it means that the precise succession of episodes is essential in a story, otherwise it is not the same story at all. Now if one performs rituals in order to achieve certain results (which, after all, is the point of most rituals) or if one tells certain stories because they contain important truths, one will be led to insist on accurate repetition and to worry about the smallest changes. One's behaviour in such circumstances will be much more like that of the computer scientists than that of the political 'conservatives'.

To sum up: the reformed conception assumes that 'conservatism' is the cause of traditional literalism; but if there is any causal relation here, it is very likely to go in the opposite direction. It is because people consider the surface properties of traditional phenomena as essential that they tend to favour their exact repetition. Describing this as 'conservatism' is very misleading; even if people display some 'conservatism', this cannot be the cause of repetition. Lots of things get repeated without people being conservative about them; indeed, lots of aspects of traditional interaction get repeated because people do not remember anything else. In such cases it is memory itself that makes the selection, a point the implications of which I will examine presently.

Let me now summarise the state of the argument. The common conception of traditions relies on two main assumptions: (i) that traditional interaction is structured by underlying conceptions and world-views; (ii) that its repetition is caused by people's conservatism. Assuming that people are conservative about underlying conceptions is just untenable. If, on the other hand, we say that they are 'conservative' about surface properties, we therefore abandon the first claim. But then we get another problem: the intentional view of repetition is based on a distortion of ethnographic facts and a strange view of human memory. If a hypothesis generates so many problems it should be discarded, unless it is the only one available. Anthropological discussions often convey the impression that conservatism about underlying conceptions or conservatism about literal execution are the only possible explanations of traditional repetition. But that is not the case; another reasonable hypothesis can be put forward. In the following pages I will show that it is less expensive, in terms of additional hypotheses and implicit psychology; in the rest of the book I will argue that it explains more.

Repetition and the representation of interaction

How can we explain traditional repetition without having the same problems as the common and reformed conceptions? Since most problems come from the intentional view of repetition, it seems reasonable to begin by examining the alternative, that is, the idea that repetition is an automatic process, out of people's control. The implication is that, given certain conditions, some forms of social interaction are such that they will be reproduced, while others will just disappear. The problem, obviously, is to describe the 'conditions' in question. Let me first observe that the idea of an automatic process, which conserves certain cultural traits and discards others, is not especially new; in fact, most evolutionary models of culture are based on the hypothesis of some such process, adaptive or otherwise, which 'selects' certain cultural traits. The analogy with natural selection is constant, although it is not always clearly understood (Ingold 1986: 33ff).

Here we are not concerned with these long-term processes, but with the more modest task of explaining why an occurrence of a certain social interaction displays surface features which are similar to previous occurrences, and how the previous occurrences provide the guidelines for subsequent performances. Obviously, the device that performs the selection is human memory. The intentional view of traditional repetition implies, as we saw above, a strong and implausible claim about human memory. An automatic view will imply some such claims, too; it will imply, for instance, that memory should be considered as a *filter* or some kind of sieve.[11] Human memory imposes definite constraints on the material processed. It cannot stock just *any* format of representations. Furthermore, it does not retrieve all types of representations with the same success. Some types of ideas are easier to store and retrieve than others because of the built-in specifications of individual memory, so that they are more likely to be conserved and therefore to be traditional.

The hypothesis seems to provide a simple explanation of repetition; the aspects of interaction which get repeated are the memorable ones. Stated in these terms, however, the hypothesis is true simply because it is tautological. What is repeated in a certain culture must have been memorised, and what is memorised must be more memorable than what was forgotten. That it is more memorable is demonstrated by the fact that it is better memorised. The explanation is bound to remain circular, unless some psychological hypotheses specify the general constraints brought to bear on the ideas memorised. To take but one example, it is perfectly possible to specify the constraints that make certain stories more memorable than others. This type of inquiry, initiated by Bartlett, is based on an experimental study of the memorisation of stories. By varying the format of the experimental material, and observing the resulting differences in memorisation, it is possible to put forward a formal description of the difference between 'good' (i.e., memorable) stories and 'bad' ones. Not surprisingly, the stories collected in the field turn out, in most cases, to conform to the structural constraints drawn from the laboratory experiments.[12] This just implies that in the process of transmission, stories are either modified towards a 'good' format, or simply forgotten. The moral of this example is that, if we have a set of precise cognitive hypotheses about the memorisation of cultural phenomena, we can have precise, non-question-begging hypotheses about their repetition. We will then be able to interpret traditional myth as made of particularly memorable stories, traditional ritual as particularly memorable sequences of gestures and actions, and so on. So the theory of traditions, if it is based on precise cognitive claims, will be both anthropologically significant (it will predict things that actually happen, and those it rules out will not be observed) and psychologically plausible.

There are some problems, however, to do with the assumptions of the theory. We have two hypotheses here: (i) that the requirements of human memory are the cause of effective memorisation (this is the automatic repetition stance) and (ii) that this is all we need to account for the repetition of traditional interaction. In order that we can proceed from (i) to (ii), however, another assumption is necessary, namely (iii) that all the repeated aspects of the interaction are mentally represented. Otherwise the explanation will not work. In other words, if some aspects of social interaction are not mentally represented, then *ipso facto* they cannot be memorised. Now if they cannot be memorised, the workings of human memory surely cannot have any effect on their repetition. So if we want human memory to be the cause of the repetition of interaction, than we must assume that the interaction is entirely represented.

Whether traditional interaction is represented, or more precisely, whether all the relevant repeated aspects are represented, is an empirical question. Some forms of interaction are entirely represented, some are not. To take but simple examples, playing a string quartet may be a social interaction in which all relevant aspects of the interaction are represented by all participants; each of them knows his or her score, the others' score and (roughly) the resulting musical effect. On the other hand, the daily traffic jams on the motorways near a large city certainly display a recurrent pattern. Explaining the repetition in this case does not imply assuming that the recurrent patterns are represented in anybody's mind. Chances are good that there is a continuum between such extreme cases. So where is traditional interaction? This question is crucial because, if it is at the same end of the spectrum as chamber music, then it is entirely represented and a 'filter' view of human memory is all we need to account for traditional repetition. If it is at the other end, then whatever refined models we have of human memory will not constitute a sufficient explanation of traditional repetition. Here I will argue that it is somewhere in between, which of course does not sound like a very audacious or promising claim. But it is somewhere in between in an interesting way, that is, the combination of represented and non-represented elements is not entirely haphazard and its description is crucial to our understanding of repetition. As a result, hypotheses about memorisation will play a major role in my account of traditional phenomena, but the 'filter' function of individual memory will not be considered the cause of their repetition, only an important background condition.

Events, communications and repetition

Let me now abandon the rigid deductions, and introduce some speculative claims that will be substantiated only in the course of this book. Most of the traditional phenomena we want to explain constitute *communicative events*, i.e., events whose representation by the different participants differ in a non-trivial, principled manner. Communicative events can be generally character-ised as involving different actors, and inducing some changes in at least some participants' representations. This of course is both vague and minimal, but these trivial characteristics of communication have important consequences here. If the events considered have any cognitive effects, it is *because* the representations available to different participants are different.

To make this less abstract, let me return once again to Fang epics. There is a clear-cut distinction between certain events labelled 'mvet sessions' and other events. The principles of the distinction, however, are not entirely accessible to the actors, because a mvet session implies people's participation in many different ways; as a consequence, people's representations of the mvet vary from person to person in a non-trivial way. The composition of the audience, for instance, is not entirely immaterial. When singing about his initiation, the poet makes elaborate allusions to various rituals, of which only few listeners have some knowledge. These competent listeners typically engage in some informal and highly metaphorical dialogues with the singer; their contribution is indispensable, as is that of the other listeners. Such dialogues not only imply a strict distribution of ritual knowledge, they also display it, and this complex interaction between those who know, those who don't and those who know who knows what, is essential for a good mvet session (see Boyer 1984, 1988). This is an organised partition; if the listeners' representations were randomly distributed, or if everyone had much the same

20

ideas about ancestors and witchcraft, the communicative effect would not be achieved.

This of course is a limiting case, in the sense that knowledge and its distribution are what a mvet session is all about. But the remark would apply to other forms of interaction, and I think (this is where speculation begins) that it would in fact apply to most forms of traditional interaction. The salient instances anthropologists study nearly always comprise some specific allocation of roles. To return to the example mentioned at the beginning of this chapter, the newly initiated shaman is telling colleagues and other villagers about his journeys to the world of the spirits. This is a form of interaction in which a specific allocation of roles is certainly crucial; the new shaman does certain things *qua* new shamans, the senior ones *qua* senior shamans, and so on. So far, nothing but obvious features of interaction. The hypothesis I will try to defend, however, goes further. The idea is that: (i) there are differences between the various participants' representations of the interaction; (ii) these differences are *principled*; and (iii) they are a *causal factor* in the repetition of the interaction. I do not think the first point needs much justification; the idea is, for example, that the new shaman certainly does not have the same representation of the singing session as the senior shamans. The main idea, however, is that such differences, beyond individual and other trivial ones, are organised and that their distribution has consequences for repetition. That is, the way a new shaman's representation of the singing differs from that of the senior shamans is a crucial element of the interaction, without which there would be no repetition.

It is worthwhile insisting a little on this question, if only to distinguish necessary platitudes and important hypotheses. The platitude is that there *are* some differences between the participants' representations. A semi-platitude, as it were, is the idea that these differences are *organised*, they are not just the result of personal capacities and interests. The main hypothesis is that these organised differences are among the causes of traditional repetition; admitting this has obvious consequences in the empirical study of traditional interaction. If we think that these differences are unprincipled or trivial, then we will be led to study, e.g., the shaman's initiation ceremony in terms of shared representations about the interaction. We will insist on those 'ideas' which are present in most participants' minds, judging the differences as either unprincipled (there is no organised distribution) or irrelevant (their presence does not change traditional repetition). If, on the other hand, we think that the differences in representations are principled and causally relevant for repetition, we will be led to focus on the way certain representations are not shared by the participants. This, I will claim, is the right direction; neglecting this possibility has led anthropology to put forward insufficient accounts of traditional repetition.

To make things more intuitive, there is all the difference in the world between explaining a string quartet's performance and explaining a game of cards. In the former case, all you need in order to explain why these people produce organised sound, not random noise, is a description of shared representations about the score and each player's part in it. If you want to explain the point of a card game, you need a set of hypotheses about both shared information (the knowledge of the rules for instance) and the precise way some of the information is not shared (the knowledge of one's hand). Anthropologists have generally neglected the possibility that some forms of social interaction may be closer to the latter type, except in cases where the principled differences jumped at them, as it were, for example in cases where secrecy and mystery were the actors' main preoccupations. Such cases stand out because people are aware of the differences and their organising principles; my claim is just that, in many other forms, possibly all forms of traditional interaction, there are organised differences of which the actors are not necessarily aware, and that they play a major role in the process of repetition.

Conclusion

Here I have tried to discuss at some length the 'common' claims made about traditional repetition. At least one point should now be clear: although they seem self-evident, almost trivial, these claims are immensely problematic. They fail to constitute a coherent, empirically significant account of repetition. The confusion lies, not in the solutions put forward, but in the terms of the question. The actual repetition of occurrences of social interaction is replaced with the hypothesised conservation of world-views. The fact that traditional material is necessarily memorised is just ignored, and human memory is considered as a neutral, user-controlled storage mechanism. In lieu of empirical hypotheses, what is thus offered is a series of question-begging devices.

It is possible, however, to go beyond these claims, and to treat traditional repetition as the object of precise, explanatory hypotheses. So far I have only argued for the *possibility* of such a theory, without making any substantial hypotheses. I have thus replaced the imaginary 'solutions' to a largely artificial problem, with a real, empirical problem which has no solution so far. Certain forms of social interaction lead to the repetition of their surface aspects. The crucial claim is that, all else being equal, the cause of the repetition is to be found in people's representation of these surface aspects; more precisely, in the way these representations are distributed among participants.

The only way to substantiate this claim is to put forward a series of specific, empirically significant hypotheses about various traditional inter-actions, and then to measure to what extent these aspects or their combination contribute to the repetition of the interaction considered. This is what I will do in the following chapters. I will consider tradition as a *type of interaction which results in the repetition of certain communicative events.* That tradition is a form of interaction, that it concerns communication and results in repetition are all rather obvious features, which are usually obscured by vague 'theoretical' statements about conservatism and other such properties. In this book I will try and account for several general characteristics of traditional interaction. I hope it will at least show that, as I said at the beginning, the study of tradition is a matter for explicit, substantial hypotheses rather than vague conceptual deductions.

2

How to think with 'empty' notions

The translation or gloss of specific cultural categories is an important aspect of anthropological description. It is therefore appropriate to begin our survey of traditional interaction and its psychological conditions by some remarks on concepts and categories. Describing local categories is more often than not a difficult task, for reasons both trivial and important. Some terms designate institutions which are just absent from the anthropologist's world (e.g. 'potlatch') so that the gloss must comprise some description of the referent; such difficulties are easily overcome. In this chapter, however, I will focus on the thorny problems posed by some fundamental categories of traditional ritual. They seem crucial in the description of whole systems of representations and interaction; yet their interpretation in anthropological theories is extremely problematic.

The analysis of local categories is usually considered an excellent approach, at least as a starting point, in the description of social interaction. Obviously, the description of social interaction cannot but mention the categories actually used by the participants; there is simply no way to describe, e.g., the interaction of shamans and their clients without considering their notion of 'spirits' or 'souls', or some fertility rituals without a notion of 'ancestors', as the case may be. Not to put too fine a point on it, categories should be described because their use is part of the interaction described. People use them, argue about them, and so on. There is a second, more interesting reason why anthropologists examine local categories, namely, that their representation in people's minds includes some important assumptions about the entities designated. To put it crudely, concepts seem to carry implicit theories, or some elements of the theories. In order to describe Fang ideas about death, it may be useful to start with a gloss of the term *bekong*, (roughly) translatable as 'ghosts'. By providing a detailed, fine-grained gloss of the term, we will inevitably evoke some important local ideas about death and life and bodies and minds. This surely will not be enough, but it is a good start.[1]

It may be important to examine the implicit assumptions in this study of local categories, which sometimes leads to implausible theoretical statements.

24

Remember that anthropologists, in order to describe traditional interaction, must take some hypotheses about (i) what representations people have, and (ii) the way these representations make it possible for them to participate in the interaction. The description of categories is therefore crucial, because (i) they are necessarily the object of some mental representations, and (ii) such representations cannot be just individual fantasies. It is generally assumed that local categories are *mentally defined*, and that their definitions are *shared* between users. There does not seem to be anything controversial (or indeed, anything worth dwelling on) in such assumptions. In normal conditions, one may assume that a speaker uses terms like 'giraffe' and 'hairdresser' because he or she has some representations of what giraffes and hairdressers are; one may also assume that people can use 'giraffe' and 'hairdresser' in conversations because they share a good part of these representations. In other words, if we are looking for shared mental representations, categories are the domain in which we can safely assume we will find them.

In this chapter I will focus on cases where the analysis of local categories, based on these assumptions, meets difficult problems. In such cases, two alternatives are open: (i) we may judge that the description of the shared representations is wrong or incomplete, should be further refined, etc.; (ii) or else we must assume that there is something wrong with the very idea of shared mental definitions. I will present an ethnographic example, some aspects of which are in fact very common in traditional contexts. I will then examine to what extent such cases lead to a revision of the common assumptions about categories and their use.

A Fang category and a general problem

The Fang notion of *evur* is generally glossed in the anthropological literature as 'witchcraft substance' or 'witchcraft organ'. Evur is a central notion in Fang ritual and in the beliefs concerning witchcraft, medicine, and more generally, individual capacities.[2] Only some people have evur; this enables them to get rich, to avoid misfortune or 'send' it to others, to kill people by witchcraft, to become epic-singers and witch-doctors, etc.; on the other hand, people fall ill or die either because 'their' evur is attacked by someone else's, or because they are without evur and therefore defenceless.

The domain of evur extends beyond 'witchcraft'; evur is supposed to be instrumental in all varieties of personal achievement and in every event that is not related to the system of lineage hierarchy. There is a strong opposition in Fang discourse between the 'village' order, organised by kinship ties, and the domain of the 'forest' where evur is dominant. This opposition is also that of day and night, order and disorder, cooperation and selfishness, etc. Such personal achievements as becoming a famous epic-singer or a powerful orator are always interpreted as the result of some 'nightly', evur-related action. The assumption is that successful people are *beyem*, i.e., evur-bearers; their evur sucks up other people's blood, ruins their plantations, and generally undermines their endeavours. Success is always acquired through someone else's demise, and it is interpreted as the irruption of evur powers in the otherwise fair and peaceful village world.

The notion is intrinsically ambiguous. Describing it as an 'organ' is insufficient, though sometimes pertinent. The Fang used to perform post-mortems, when they thought a person had died as a result of his or her involvement in witchcraft activities. When a polypus was found in the intestines, it was identified as the evur of the deceased; but the absence of such a salient trace was not a clear proof of innocence. The term does not designate the 'organ' itself, which is only a manifestation of evur; nor does it denote the special capacities. Specifically, it denotes whatever gives some people those special capacities. Analysing this notion is difficult because people have extremely vague views on what evur exactly consists of and the mechanisms of its action. People are quite definite, on the other hand, on such topics as the type of effects evur has, the social relations that revolve around evur-related actions, the dangers of dealing with evur-bearers, and so on; but they cannot say what evur is.

Notions like evur are extremely common in traditional interaction. Almost every anthropologist has, in the course of fieldwork, come across such a term, which is extremely ambiguous, yet is placed at the very heart of traditional discourse. In anthropological descriptions, such terms are often translated as 'vital force' or 'mystical energy'. Some people are said to 'have' it, while others do not. Informants will readily claim that the 'x' in question is a good, evil, necessary, powerful, dangerous thing, they will easily describe the social relationships and ritual acts connected with the 'x', the persons supposed to know about such things, but they seem unable to define what the 'x' is. Such notions constitute a limiting case for anthropological hypotheses. Although they are of constant use in the traditions concerned, their exact meaning seems to remain obscure or inscrutable to the speakers themselves.

This combination of extreme salience and apparent vacuity constitutes a challenge to the common anthropological ideas about traditional categories. We started with the seemingly plausible idea that categories imply shared definitions. Here we are dealing with notions which do not seem to be defined at all, yet are constantly used in a traditional interaction. Indeed, one could contend that there is a direct relation between the vagueness or even vacuity of the terms and their use in traditional symbolism. Even if we do not take this as a causal relation, the correlation is striking. In most traditional contexts there is some notion of that kind; and it is usually among the fundamental notions, without which there can be no description of the interaction concerned.[3] But then the idea of shared definitions as the basis of traditions is clearly threatened. So we must examine in more detail how anthropology tries to cope with such odd categories.

Two anthropological approaches

There are, ideally, two ways of dealing with local categories which seem impossible to define, while maintaining that categories are the object of shared definitions. A first strategy consists in saying that the categories are indeed undefined, but that they are an exceptional case. Alternatively, one can assume that the notions in question are not undefined, but that their description is incomplete, because anthropologists have just been looking for the wrong kind of definition.

The first approach was defended by C. Levi-Strauss in his analysis of the Melanesian notion of *mana*. From the 1910s to the 1940s, this notion was a *locus classicus* of anthropological discussions. The notion was used as a paradigm of magical thought; the very notion of mana is the point of departure in Marcel Mauss's famous *Esquisse d'une theorie de la magie*. This purely theoretical discussion subsisted for several decades on its abstract level, without much consideration for the new data gathered. In a general survey of the theories about mana, Keesing (1984) showed that anthropologists consistently ignored the linguistic or discursive evidence, and based most of their interpretation on a substantive use of the term ('*the mana*'), which simply does not exist in the languages concerned.[4]

Discussions about mana had somewhat subsided when C. Levi-Strauss wrote his 'Introduction a l'oeuvre de Marcel Mauss' (Mauss 1951, and in Levi-Strauss 1987), in which he argues that notions like mana are universal ('une forme de pensee universelle et permanente') and offers a simple linguistic explanation. Mana-concepts are taken as central cultural symbols not *in spite of* but *because of* their semantic vacuity. They must be considered as 'a zero symbolic value', to be compared with phonological 0−features (1987: 64). They can also be compared to algebraic symbols, which are in themselves devoid of meaning, but can be precisely used to denote any number. Levi-Strauss offers yet a third analogy; mana-concepts resemble the French words *truc* and *machin* (or the English 'stuff'), generally used to denote any object for which the speaker does not find an accurate name or description (1987: 55). For Levi-Strauss, this common usage gives us the key to the symbolic elaboration on mana notions. The argument can be summed up as follows:

(i) the construal of the world implicit in linguistic categorisation does not entirely fit with human knowledge of the world;
(ii) hence the need for a special signifier which encompasses whatever knowledge 'stick out' of the linguistic framework;
(iii) this 'empty signifier' denotes virtually anything, precisely because it is meaningless.[5]

This ingenious explanation is consonant with a general structuralist idea of categories as forming a 'grid' of 'signifiers'. Terms like *truc* and *machin*, and traditional categories like mana, are all-purpose signifiers that designate whatever 'sticks out' of the structural grid. I will not comment on the grand claims about human thought and language; their vagueness would make the discussion difficult in any case. But we must focus on the specific hypothesis made about traditional categories like 'mana' or 'evur', namely that they are 'empty notions' which denote just whatever one has no word for.

If we try to apply this idea to any particular case, it becomes clear that the *truc* analogy just flies in the face of the facts. Traditional categories are precisely *not* used in that way. They are not used as the joker in cards. First, the languages in which they occur generally have some other means to cope with 'signifieds without signifiers', for things one has no word for. Most natural languages do provide some 'joker cards', but these are never confused with the traditional categories we are dealing with. To take but one example, a Fang mechanic who has no Fang word for 'differential gear' calls it *dzom ete* (this stuff), and certainly not 'evur'. Conversely, it is obvious that traditional categories are used in a very precise way. Intuitive rules govern the use of such terms, and the ethnographer's job is to make them explicit. If such rules did not exist, if the categories actually denoted anything, then it would be in principle impossible to tell a serious use of the term from mere gibberish. But the ethnographers' informants are usually able to make such a distinction, which suggests that there must be some limits to the use of the categories.

Although ingenious, Levi-Strauss's *truc* analogy is clearly wrong; in order to go beyond such explanations, however, it is important to examine the assumptions on which the explanation is based. The main idea is that the study of local categories should be directed at language, conceived as an abstract system of interrelated symbols, not at the way language is represented and used by speakers. Seen at that abstract level, there may well be some resemblance between *mana* and *truc*. All the empirical objections to the *truc* analogy concern the representation and use of the categories. The intuitive rules the ethnographers try to uncover concern the use of the term. Hence no solution to this question can be found unless one considers, not only the position of the terms in the vocabulary, but also their use in people's utterances.[6]

Let me now turn to the second alternative, in which it is assumed that terms like 'evur' are problematic because their description is incomplete. Anthropologists report that it is very difficult to elicit any definition of such terms; the apparent 'vacuity' seems an essential aspect of the notions. Without challenging this, it may be possible to argue that anthropologists are mistaken about the status of such terms. A typical example of such an argument is the 'neo-intellectualist' conception mentioned in chapter 1. In this framework, tradition as a whole is considered as an attempt to reach a theoretical understanding of the world. Horton thus compares the gods and spirits of African cosmologies to the 'hidden' entities of modern scientific explanations, such as waves and electrons. Both kinds of concepts are used to place events in a 'wider causal context', and to achieve 'explanation, prediction and control' of certain contingencies. The comparison seems to apply even better in the case of mana notions, although Horton does not discuss them; mana or evur or other such 'things' could then be considered as theoretical principles, and that would explain why they are impersonal and causative entities. No one can really explain what evur is, no more than modern physicists would explain what electro-magnetism is. But to suppose that such a hidden 'thing' exists and brings about certain effects is the only way to account for many events. The hypothesis is part of a theory, and in Horton's framework traditional categories are names which designate principles described or explained in certain theories about the world.

There are obvious advantages to this interpretation, especially in contrast with the structuralist claims. The intellectualist paradigm makes it possible to take into account the obvious fact that there *are* some constraints on the use of these categories. The explanation is that the terms cannot be used as 'jokers' because the implicit theory fixes their reference; not every phenomenon fits into the theory. A set of theoretical principles determine what is and what is not an electron; in much the same way, for a 'neo-intellectualist', there must be a traditional theory which explains what is and what is not evur or mana. There are some obvious problems, however, with this type of 'explanation'. First of all, a limited problem of concept representation is 'solved' by creating a much bigger problem elsewhere, in the representation of theories. Not to put too fine a point on it, the arguments developed in chapter 1 should suggest that it is not absolutely self-evident that people entertain 'theories' about such things as evur. The utterances they produce about this topic are mostly about singular situations; they do not display or even imply consistent explanatory principles. Theories about evur, if there are such things in the minds of Fang people, are unconscious and not really consistent. So we have to admit that, if these ideas are called 'theories', then we should waive the requirements of consistency and explicitness usually applied to theories. Having 'a theory of evur' will then mean having organised thoughts about evur.[7]

This, however, is a self-defeating argument. In this discussion, the only advantage of the idea of traditional 'theories' was that it seemed to explain how people can have a precise use of a term without a definition. Now if the theory is vague or inconsistent, how could it put any constraints on the use of the term? If people's 'theories' about evur, for instance, are inconsistent then they are of no help in using the term; they do not provide any guidelines. The idea of traditional 'theories', in the explanation of traditional notions, leads to the same dilemmas as in the explanation of traditional repetition. The claim is either strong (the term 'theory' is taken in its clear, usual sense) and implausible, or watered down to fit the data and consequently trivial.

There is a common point in the structuralist and 'intellectualist' approaches. Instead of considering actual uses of a notion, these approaches focus on abstract objects, either the system of 'signifieds' or the traditional 'theory'. As a result, it is implied that the use of terms like 'evur' is simple, and can be derived from the abstract objects considered. In the structuralist approach, making an utterance about 'evur' only involves some knowledge about the language. In the intellectualist model, it only involves knowing the relevant theory. In order to go beyond these problematic hypotheses, it may be necessary to examine the way such terms as 'evur' are used in actual communication. Against the models presented here, I would claim that we must distinguish between several interrelated 'registers' or 'styles' of discourse. These distinctions, sometimes explicit, are never ignored by people who use the terms. My account will be based upon the Fang data, but I think many ethnographers will recognise situations they often deal with.

Evur and discourse registers

There are many types of discourse about evur, which is a very common topic of conversation among the Fang. The first and most important source of ethnographic material is people's informal conversations and assertions, what I will call *common discourse*. At the beginning of this chapter I mentioned some properties of evur; all these were taken from common discourse. To take but one example of the contexts of common discourse, people often evoke, in casual conversations, the alleged increase of witchcraft murders which is seen as a consequence of the colonisation and the destruction of former ancestor cults. On such occasions, people seldom fail to mention the general characteristics of evur. It has 'neither back nor stomach', i.e., it is ambiguous, no-one can really grasp it or know the truth about it. Evur is a 'thing of the forest', it belongs to the uncanny world of the bush and the night, away from the order and daylight of the village. Some 'selfish' people use evur, and it is a pity one cannot tell them from harmless villagers. When an evur-bearer is asleep, he or she in fact goes to *mgbel*, a forest village where all witches meet and fight. These fights typically result in illness, as a person's evur is weakened or wounded in mgbel.

These assertions are very general and abstract. Few singular examples are given, and the origin of this knowledge is always attributed to the ancestors: 'the elders knew all about evur', 'they told us about that', etc. There are no formalised circumstances for this kind of speech, neither is the audience 'restricted' in any sense. Anyone can hear what the 'common wisdom' has to say about evur. However, no one can draw any definite conclusions from this type of discourse, which is often vague and contradictory. The conception of evur that emerges from these casual statements is that anything is possible as far as evur is concerned, so that any definite straightforward statement should be indefinitely qualified. The speakers themselves always assume that they are not knowledgeable enough to be precise and definite. Many assertions are thus followed by the speaker's self-evaluation: 'this is what I've been told, but after all I'm not a *ngengang* (witch-doctor)', 'I tell you what I've heard, but who can be sure about such things?', and so on. So common discourse can be characterised as (i) generalising; (ii) not related to any precisely defined source of knowledge; and (iii) willingly unconclusive.

These features are virtually inverted in a second type of discourse about evur, in gossip about witchcraft. This second form only occurs in the context of private conversations. The adressee is not, of course, a 'general audience', he or she is chosen carefully. Gossip never uses general assertions; on the contrary it is focused on singular cases and the only generalisations are implicit. What is even more important, it is always assumed that the speaker has a definite interest in transmitting a certain version of the events. This is why people constantly remind each other not to trust people who engage in gossip, although people actually do it as often as possible, and important decisions are based on information gathered in such conversations. Witchcraft cases are sometimes brought before the weekly customary courts; when pleading their cases, many people must resort to information acquired through gossip. They often try to present it as direct evidence, the origin of which they do not want to disclose; for instance, they 'know' a certain person has performed a certain ritual, but they will not clearly state that they *saw* it. Every time gossip information is mentioned *as such*, it is instantly dismissed as 'empty talk' or 'lies'; it is rejected on *formal* grounds. On the contrary, any assertion that is presented as personal testimony is either accepted or argued against on account of its *content*.

Gossip is just as inconclusive as common discourse; in every single case of witchcraft one can hear many incompatible versions through gossip, and one can very well relate each version to the speaker's own interests. Furthermore, it is virtually impossible to use knowledge acquired through gossip in any context other than gossip itself, because this would result in personal accusations. In short, gossip is (i) very definite, (ii) centered on singular cases and (iii) of no use in the contexts in which truths are supposedly expressed.

Most common statements about evur, either private or public, general or particular, are supposedly unreliable. There is, however, another register in which definite statements can be found, namely that of the 'experts'. These include not only witch-doctors but other kinds of healers, and diviners as well. These people have to make statements about evur, whenever they are requested to give a supposedly competent opinion on a certain case or event. The statements can be made in private or in public. It is common, for instance, for people to organise a session of divination shortly after a death, and this session is public.

On such an occasion an expert often resorts to general principles which can be found in common discourse, but he also makes a definite statement about the singular case. For instance, a diviner says: 'you all know that evur is of the forest, is an evil thing. Those who engage in things of the forest eventually have to pay dearly for it,' etc., However, these pedestrian remarks are but a prelude to the 'real' statement, about the problem in hand. In the same way, a witch-doctor usually proceeds from abstract commonplaces to a graphic explanation of what is wrong with a certain person, on which side of the family the origin of the problem is, etc. In such utterances, there is no clear conceptual connection between the general principles and the singular case. Although the expert presents his conclusions as a mere deduction from the propositions of common discourse, it is clear to all laymen that only experts could come to these conclusions and make such statements; this impression is reinforced by the amount of details mentioned by the expert, as a simple example will show.

In a Fang village where I worked I once heard that a young boy I knew was seriously ill, and I was requested to give some 'tablets', which proved as ineffective as those provided by the dispensary. When all other possibilities were exhausted, the family took the boy to a famous specialist of evur witchcraft, who asserted that the illness had begun during a recitation of epic stories I had organised. According to the healer, it should have been noticed that there were many ants crossing the house where the story-telling session was taking place, and also that the epic singer had put out his tongue several times, for no obvious reason. The final diagnosis was that the boy's evur was strong and malevolent, so that he could not stand the presence of another evur-bearer, the epic singer in the case at hand. This also explained the latter's 'agressive' reaction. Everyone found the explanation quite satisfactory; ants and anthills are commonly associated with witchcraft and, for the Fang, sticking out one's tongue is an agressive and uncanny gesture.

The experts know how to apply the general principles (e.g., about evur, ant-hills, etc.) in a pertinent way, a capacity which is guaranteed by their special initiation. The problem with this interplay of general principles and specific cases is that the experts' utterances cannot be generalised, except by the experts themselves. The statements are memorised literally, with all the contextual details of the case. For all these reservations, one must admit that such diagnoses are an important source of reliable information about evur. To put it briefly, the experts' utterances are (i) definite, (ii) focused on singular cases and (iii) fairly reliable.

Discourse and shared representations

Let me now try to draw some general conclusions from this ethnographic example. Although some notion of 'witchcraft power', more or less similar to 'evur', can be found in many traditional contexts, I will not pursue this point here. The hypotheses I want to put forward concern the discursive properties of the term, the way its use is distributed in different discourse registers. In the Fang case, we have three main types of discourse about evur: common discourse is generalising but inconclusive, gossip is definite but unreliable, expert discourse is definite and reliable. This rough division, based on the type of information that is conveyed and its reliability, is congruent with a division between types of context. Obviously, many aspects of this tripartite division are particular to Fang culture. There is a formal property, however, which seems to be a general feature of traditional interaction, and therefore deserves more attention.

Although I have drawn a division between three types of discourse, there is an obvious difference between gossip and common discourse on the one hand, and expert discourse on the other. The difference concerns the *reliability* of the information conveyed. While gossip and common discourse provide listeners with relevant material, expert utterances are supposed to convey true information. As I mentioned, this information is only about a singular situation, it is nonetheless conceived as guaranteed truth. That there is a difference between unreliable registers on the one hand, and the truth-delivering one on the other, is clear in the difference of cognitive salience. Gossip and common discourse utterances, although they are often extremely relevant and interesting, are never the object of so much inference and comment as expert discourse. Also, expert utterances are not easily forgotten. They are quoted and commented on long after the corresponding situation has changed. They focus people's attention much more than other forms of discourse.

This division, I will claim, is an important general property of traditional interaction. The fundamental categories of such interactions are used in many types of discourse. There is, however, a principled difference between registers in which reliable information is conveyed, and the rest. In the analysis of traditional notions, one can make use of two types of data: the inferences that can be drawn from ordinary conversations, allusions, etc., on the one hand, and some salient utterances, made in specific contexts by specific speakers on the other. Whatever the idiom in which the distinction is expressed, and however subtle the differences made within each domain, there is a sharp division between registers of discourse in which speakers are supposed to refer to what the entities really are, and registers for which there is no such guarantee.

This general hypothesis, taken on its own, is not really controversial. Most anthropological descriptions mention this type of distinction, between contexts in which truths are produced about the fundamental categories, and contexts in which information is conveyed without any guarantee of truth. Although uncontroversial, the idea has some important consequences. As I said at the beginning, the main reason why categories are supposed to give access to local 'conceptions' is that one assumes there must be shared definitions of the categories. The idea of a division between registers, however, makes it necessary to modify this seemingly trivial hypothesis.

Reliable, guaranteed utterances are not made by everyone; the experts, in traditional contexts, are precisely identified speakers. Now this implies that some aspects of the representations concerned are, precisely, *not* shared by all members of the group. More importantly, it implies that these aspects are crucial to any description of the interaction. To return to the Fang example, an analysis of the shared aspects of the representation of 'evur' would not give any insight into the social interaction concerned. The representations shared by everyone are the basis of common discourse, which, as I said, is not especially salient. If, on the other hand, we want to understand the use of 'evur' in salient interaction, then we must focus on expert utterances; but then we are dealing with a type of context in which the interlocutors have strikingly different representations about the notion, as we will see presently. The difference between expert discourse and other registers cannot be explained as a difference in *definitions*, so that we must revise the second fundamental hypothesis in the anthropological treatment of traditional categories.

The acquisition of a 'mystical' notion

The three types of discourse about evur are obviously interrelated. Gossip assertions are based upon some general premises that can be found in common discourse, and they often mention cases that have been investigated by an expert; common discourse is often a result of what people have learned through either gossip or experts' assertions. But these different types of discourse are not simply juxtaposed, they are *ordered*, both logically and chronologically. Expert discourse is conceived as something that goes beyond common talk or gossip. For the Fang, to be an expert is to have 'other eyes to see the hidden resemblance of things', i.e., something *more* than other people. Moreover, the levels of discourse are ordered chronologically, as one can become an expert only by going through a long initiation; hence people who become witch-doctors or diviners have handled gossip and common discourse before acquiring their expertise. As a consequence, the process of acquisition is crucial for our description of people's representations about the notion. It is an initiation process, the details of which vary according to the specialised activity one wants to reach. But the general framework is essentially the same.

Let us take the example of witch-doctors or *ngengang*. The initiation is a strictly individual process. It begins when the ngengang-to-be is taken ill, or receives other signs which mean that he or she has an evur. But evur in itself is ambiguous and consequently dangerous even for the bearer. It must be 'shaped' (*akoma*) so as to bring about its bearer's well-being without his or her engaging in witchcraft. This is achieved through a ritual which is the first step in the initiation process. After the 'revelation' of the presence of evur, the process is variable; one can become a healer's apprentice, and learn many recipes and treatments by 'buying' them from one's master. But the crucial steps in the process are rituals which involve the neophyte's symbolic death and his encounter with ancestors or forest spirits. In these rituals the initiate has to explore the world of the ancestors and bring back the *byang*, the secrets that will enable him/her to practice as a ngengang.

In his remarkably detailed account of Fang witchcraft and magic, L. Mallart-Guimera gives several examples of such apprenticeship; let me summarise one of these (see Mallart-Guimera 1981: 158–88). Laurent Bikoe's initiation begins with a serious disease, a dysenteric infection which lasts for several years and brings him close to death. After consulting many experts, including Pygmy doctors, he meets Ngono, a famous healer who tells him he has been 'sent' the 'oil-of-the-ghost', i.e., he is a victim of that specific form of witchcraft which makes one's blood turn black and thick. One night, in a series of dreams, he meets his ancestors who give him marrow seeds to eat, and order him to 'go and cure people', to 'make the byang' (the medicines). Laurent is soon cured of the dysentery, and learns some secrets from Ngono, who becomes his master. One day, Ngono takes Laurent to the forest and plunges him in a river. Suddenly, Laurent sees a woman ghost, the one who 'works' for Ngono. At that point Laurent's account becomes somewhat obscure; he seems to make some deal with this woman, to the effect that she begins to 'work' for him. Every time he is presented a patient, it is the ghost who 'finds' the medicine in the forest.

The healer does not say much about the origin of his technical knowledge, his pharmacopoeia. He admits that, after his dream-initiation, he was not yet a witch-doctor, because he had no special knowledge of the illnesses and plants. He claims to have acquired this knowledge during several years of apprenticeship with various healers, and also during the period of his disease and its (unsuccessful) treatments. The very idea of a medical knowledge that is not acquired through initiation is alien to Fang thought, and the notion of a 'byang' encompasses both the recipes and the individual ability to follow them successfully. Initiation to such knowledge is strictly individual; it should be no surprise that many details vary from one healer's account to another's. Some essential features, however, are always included in these accounts: (i) the ancestor, or the witches trigger the process by sending some disease or misfortune; (ii) an expert is required to reveal the exact origin of the event; (iii) the healer-to-be is cured; (iv) he or she is given the ability to cure people and also to send them illness or death; (v) he or she invariably declines the latter offer and is content with 'working for the good', which of course is much less profitable. This process concerns the development of the person's evur, the outcome of which is not necessarily the status of witch-doctor. This is why all experts of evur-related matters, e.g., diviners, epic singers undergo this type of initiation. During my field study of epic singers, I noticed that their initiation narratives were strikingly similar to those given by Mallart-Guimera's informants (Boyer 1988: 99–114). They always focused on a journey to the ghosts' villages, during which they had been given the 'byang mvet', the secrets of good story-telling, for which there had been a very dear – and of course unmentionable – price to pay (in Fang culture most outstanding capacities are supposedly 'purchased' by giving the ghosts the life of a parent).

In short, one becomes an expert of evur by going through a series of personal experiences, notably a series of direct presentations of the world in which evur is visible. Being able to make definite statements about evur and having experienced such direct presentations of the ghosts' world are two qualities that seem necessarily connected. Indeed, the Fang conceive expert discourse as a *consequence* of such experiences. It is because someone has been in such situations that he or she makes certain statements about evur. The initiation experiences themselves are a consequence of the presence of evur. One does not decide to go through a certain initiation in order to become a witch-doctor, there is no such thing as a 'career' in healing. Rather, one adapts oneself to a situation in which one's evur and its relationship with other people's evur are crucial.

In the acquisition of expert discourse, there are two parallel processes, concerning technical knowledge on the one hand, and the ritual contacts with the domain of evur on the other. The technical knowledge in itself is not about evur at all, it is only about plants and their effects, and the categorisation of symptoms. On its own, this knowledge is supposed to be insufficient. What makes certain people able to identify the effects of evur is a series of experiences. The expert does not acquire another, more refined 'definition' or 'characterisation' of evur; he or she acquires a repertoire of salient memories, which concern singular situations, not abstract principles. Most of these experiences are just unconnected with the propositions expressed in common discourse, so that becoming an expert does not involve enriching one's characterisation of the notion. On the other hand, these memories are constantly used by experts in the identification of specific situations. In particular, the resemblance between a certain situation at hand, and memories of encounters with the domain of evur, is a guideline in the expert's work.

This could be said, *mutatis mutandis*, of most 'mystical' notions used in traditional contexts. Acquiring expert discourse implies undergoing a series of specific experiences, often described as an initiation, which cannot be construed as the acquisition of a new 'definition' for the notions concerned. Such experiences do not transmit technical knowledge, although the latter *may* be acquired in parallel. The experiences, not the knowledge, make the difference between expert discourse and the rest. The case of *evur* is not really exceptional in that sense. Without anticipating the problems I will deal with in the following chapters, let me observe that it is extremely difficult to describe such acquisition processes as the transmission of information. What is acquired by the subjects is a series of salient memories, which are then used as guidelines, together with knowledge, in the evaluation of subsequent situations.[8]

Categories and their representation

Here I have tried to show that the idea of shared mental definitions of traditional categories is not really satisfactory. If we want to focus on the relevant aspects of traditional interaction, then we are led to insist on two important properties of the categories involved, namely, that the differences in their representation are a crucial aspect of the interaction, and that a good part of the representations involved do not consist in mental definitions. This I have tried to demonstrate on the basis of strictly anthropological arguments and data. It is also possible to consider this problem from a more general point of view, and to show that the common hypotheses rely on a strange idea of the way concepts and categories are represented in general. Traditional categories are, after all, but a variety of categories, so that anthropological hypotheses about the former should be compatible with what psychologists know of the latter. Principles that apply to concepts in general necessarily apply to traditional concepts. Indeed, the idea of *definitions* which are *shared* is a commonsense belief about language in general, not just traditional categories.

Commonsense it may be, but it turns out to be generally false. Both hypotheses, that categories are represented with a definition and that definitions are shared, are simply refuted in many domains of the vocabulary. Before going into the details, let me observe that the vocabulary of a natural language is not a uniform landscape, and that anthropologists should be especially aware of this. In the models I discussed above, the vocabulary was supposed to be homogeneous. In the structuralist conceptions, all there is in a vocabulary is a set of 'signifiers' with their conceptual counterparts; there are some cases of lonesome signifiers hovering around, as it were, but they are exceptional. In the intellectualist models, there are two main varieties of terms, theoretical on the one hand and non-theoretical (one guesses they must be observational) on the other. These models are just too simplistic. Even if we limit ourselves to substantives and adjectives, there are many different varieties of terms, and the idea of shared represented definitions applies only to some of them.

To have a definition, if this term has any meaning, is to have a set of necessary and sufficient conditions for an object to be a member of the class. This is possible in the case of 'triangle' and (maybe) 'hairdresser', but many terms must be used without such a list of conditions; furthermore, even in cases where it would be ideally possible to list the conditions, the hypothesis that they are mentally represented by the speakers is just untenable.[9] To take but a single example, *natural kind terms* cannot be identified by a list of necessary and sufficient conditions. Such terms denote living species and natural substances, e.g., 'giraffe', 'granite', 'oak'. The representation of these categories cannot provide a mental definition; no-one can specify the necessary and sufficient conditions for being a giraffe or an oak.[10] This example is relevant in the study of traditional categories for two reasons. First, it shows that mental definitions are out of reach in many common terms, so that seemingly 'empty' concepts like 'evur' or 'mana' are not really exceptional in that respect. Also, the comparison makes it possible to explain some important properties of traditional categories, in contrast with natural kind terms.

Terms like 'giraffe' are not represented with a definition. But people have representations that help them use the term in a meaningful way. To take a common philosophical view, people must have a certain *stereotype* of giraffes, which helps them in identifying giraffes and telling them from lions or tigers. This may consist of a mental image of a typical giraffe, or of a list of qualities which are usually found in actual giraffes. Here I will not enter the fierce psychological debates about the way stereotypes are actually represented, as this is not relevant to our problem.[11] The only important point is that a stereotype gives properties which are used to identify singular objects as members of the class, although they are neither necessary nor sufficient. Giraffes for instance may be identified because of their long neck, but exceptionally short-necked giraffes are still, unambiguously, giraffes; the property, although it is frequent, is only typical.

An interesting aspect of such categories is that one cannot acquire them by being taught the definition of the term, since there is no definition. Terms for natural kinds are usually acquired by ostension, by being shown some exemplars of the kind. Again, I will not enter the controversies about the way ostensive presentations are processed and contribute to the construction of a stereotype. All models of cognitive development share the trivial assumption, following which acquiring a natural kind term consists in memorising some ostensive presentations of exemplars of the kind, and then extrapolating a mental stereotype of the kind on the basis of that experience.[12] In other words, subjects necessarily start with particular, singular presentations and gradually build a stereotype which is (roughly) common to all speakers of the language.

The point of these remarks is, by contrast, to highlight a very important property of traditional categories, more precisely of the way expert discourse is acquired. To return to the Fang example, people do not build a stereotype out of certain presentations of evur. As I said above, such presentations are confined to some ritual contexts which can be attended to, or fully comprehended, by experts or 'experts to be'. Besides, people would not really have to 'build' the stereotype, as it mostly consists of certain vague statements that can be heard in everyday common discourse. As a result, the full acquisition of a term such as evur, i.e., the process whereby one goes beyond common discourse and achieves expertise, consists of proceeding from a stereotype (given by common discourse) to a series of ostensions (provided by the initiation contexts). In the case of natural kind terms, people have a mental representation which gradually *converges* towards the (roughly) common stereotype. The full acquisition of evur, on the other hand, starts from the stereotype and gradually *diverges* towards a series of memories of personal experiences.

To recapitulate: anthropology takes the study of local categories as an essential step in the description of traditional interaction; this much is beyond doubt. The underlying assumptions, however, are not really satisfactory. The categories used in traditional interaction are not the object of shared definitions, and understanding why and how this is the case entails some strong hypotheses about the interaction itself. Here I have put forward four main hypotheses, which I think amount to a general description of the way categories are used in traditions:

(i) there are some principled differences between discourse registers, which include a distinction between reliable 'expert' utterances and the rest;
(ii) the use of the term in different registers is based on different types of mental representations about the objects designated;
(iii) specifically, the acquisition of expert discourse relies on the memorisation of ostensive presentations;
(iv) these memories are not necessarily consistent with the stereotype.

Whether these hypotheses are true is an empirical question, which obviously cannot be answered on the basis of the ethnographic illustrations used here. But their advantage is to be both consistent with what anthropologists generally report about the use of traditional categories, and psychologically more plausible than the idea of shared mental definitions, traditional 'theories' or 'zero-signifiers'. All such claims rely on a description of concept representation and use which is simply untrue of concepts in general.

Special categories or special process?

So far I have used the term 'traditional category' in a remarkably vague way, to denote all the notions which seem to be crucial in traditional interaction.

The argument, however, relied on the example of strange categories like evur, which are fundamental in a specific tradition, yet are not easily definable and therefore challenge the common views on definitions. Let me now try to be more specific, and explain exactly what the hypotheses listed above are supposed to apply to. We have categories which are the object of a common stereotype, and of special ostensive designations, irreducible to the stereotype. The problem is, whether we are dealing here with special types of concepts, say 'undefinable mystical concepts' or 'mana-terms', or with a special process which is applied to any concept in a traditional interaction.

In the former alternative, 'mystical terms' would be considered a special variety in the vocabulary, besides such varieties as 'natural kinds', 'sensory properties', 'theoretical concepts', and so on. Traditions would be characterised by the systematic use of such 'mystical terms'.[13] If we choose the other alternative, then we will assume that any type of term can become 'mystical' in that sense, provided that there is the right type of interaction. This in fact is a general question, which is recurrent in the analysis of traditions. One has the choice, between taking the specific properties of traditions as properties of special objects, or as the application of a special process to objects that can be found in other types of interaction. In each case, I will try to show that the second option is far more plausible and satisfactory.

To return to the question of categories, it is easy to show that the hypotheses presented above apply to many notions used in traditional interaction, besides the mystical undefinable mana-like category 'evur'. This can be shown by a very brief examination of another Fang category, that of *bekong*.[14] This word is the plural form of *kong*, which usually designates a person's shadow, and is also one of the constituents of the person. After death the kong leaves the body and wanders around the village, as a rather malevolent isolated 'spirit'. Funerals contribute to 'anchor' the kong, which is then supposed to dwell in a village of bekong. The organisation and activities of such villages are similar to those of the living, although people's ideas about this are very vague. At this stage the bekong are considered rather benevolent; they are often called *betara* or *bemvam* ('fathers', 'grandfathers'). Lineage and clan cults are directed to them as protectors of the village 'order'.

People's typical image of the bekong is that of ambiguous creatures, both benevolent and uncanny. This is partly due to the fact that the ideas of 'bekong as wandering spirits' and 'bekong as fathers' are both necessarily connected (a kong is a malevolent spirit before becoming an ancestor) and not really compatible. Therefore the bekong are often described as unpredictable or whimsical; it is generally considered better to have as little to do with them as possible. The bekong can bring about various types of problems, from bad crops to serious illnesses. Before becoming 'fathers', the bekong are envious of the fun and excitement of village life. Even 'anchored' ancestors are likely to get angry when the living break the rules of normal social life, such as clan exogamy. The resulting problems make it necessary to resort to ritual experts. In much the same way as there are evur experts, some people are supposed to be particularly competent about the relationships between the village and the bekong. These experts usually are lineage elders, and they have undergone the full range of ancestor cult initiations. Their diagnoses, always focused on singular cases, are the only reliable source of information about what ancestors really are. These utterances are memorised and cited literally, and constitute a repertoire of case-stories which people use to make conjectures about present events.

At first sight, the notion of bekong seems very different from evur. For one thing, Fang speakers can always roughly define what bekong are; we are not dealing here with an apparently empty or undefinable notion. The processes involved in concept acquisition and representation, however, are very much the same. The common stereotype of ancestors does not provide, on its own, any knowledge, and therefore any way of dealing with the entities concerned. The representation of the term includes some definitional features, but these are clearly conceived as insufficient and the acquisition of the concept involves focusing on singular utterances, which ostensively designate the bekong and their action. People's general representations about the entity are insufficient if not supplemented, and virtually replaced, by memories of singular situations.

Categories and memory

The point of this chapter was to try and describe the specific features of the representation and use of categories associated with traditional contexts. My assumption was that there *are* such specific features, that categories are not used in traditions in the same way as in other contexts, for example not in the same way as in usual conversation in the societies concerned. This much is generally agreed in anthropology, but hypotheses differ a great deal about what the differences consist of. The structuralist model mentioned above has a hypothesis about such terms as 'evur' or 'mana', which is problematic for two reasons, because it is empirically untenable, and also because it implies a sharp division between 'empty signifiers' on the one hand (terms like 'evur') and 'normal' terms on the other, a class that should include terms like the Fang 'bekong'. Obviously, this is absurd; the type of interaction, the division of discourse registers and the kind of representations involved seem very much the same in the cases of 'evur' and 'bekong'.

In the intellectualist model on the other hand, 'evur' and 'bekong' would be classified together as 'theoretical' terms. This, however, is just as untenable as the structuralist interpretation, given that people's representations about 'evur' or 'bekong' just do not constitute 'theoretical' principles, unless one bends one's categories so much that 'theory' just means 'thought'. Furthermore, the intellectualist idea makes it impossible to understand the obvious difference between 'evur' and 'bekong' on the one hand, and terms like 'wavelength' and 'genotype' on the other. But the difference is obvious; no physicist has to undergo an initiation to say the truth about 'wavelengths', and no biologist would perform rituals in which 'genotype' is ostensively designated. These models provide no hypothesis about the specific features of traditional categories.

On the basis of the Fang example I have tried to show that the specific features lie in the type of representations entertained, and the way they are distributed between people who have access to different discourse registers. Traditional categories are not special *types* of categories; they are just categories represented and used in a specific way. What is interesting about such apparently empty terms as 'evur' is that they are a *limiting-case*, in which these features of the traditional process are especially visible. Not to put too fine a point on it, the main hypothesis here is that in the process of acquisition of a traditional category, the definitional features are replaced with memories of specific situations, contrary to what happens in the acquisition of most ordinary terms. This process is especially clear in the case of terms like 'evur', 'wakan', 'orenda' and other types of mystical 'forces', for which there are virtually no definitional features to begin with. But it applies just as well to ordinarily defined terms like 'ancestors'.

If this is true, then it becomes clear why anthropology is wrong in treating traditional 'event-talk' as the expression of underlying theories or conceptions. As I said in chapter 1, a notable feature of traditional discourse is the emphasis on specific situations instead of theoretical inferences, on salient examples rather than general principles. Theories of tradition have a difficult job explaining why people do not just make their 'conceptions' explicit. If traditional expert discourse is acquired in the way described here, then it is clear that the task is in fact an impossible one. Traditional interaction implies that some people supplement a vague and unconstraining common stereotype with memories of singular ostensive designations. Indeed, their discourse is generally centred on such designations and on memories of such contexts. Traditional discourse is therefore based on representations which are essentially different from common stereotypes. As a result, trying to interpret it as the *expression* of such stereotypes is not only wrong, it is like trying to put round pegs in square holes. Anthropological theories seem to identify as 'traditional' something (the expression of common stereotypes), the absence of which constitutes traditional discourse.

This strange way of dealing with traditional discourse is in fact rooted in strong, and I think misguided, claims about the psychological processes involved in the acquisition of culture in general. Here I must briefly introduce an elementary psychological distinction, between the memorisation of events as such and more general representations about the world. Having a set of representations about what took place at a certain time and location is different from having representations about the way the world is. Remembering the way so and so was dressed yesterday is not the same as remembering the French for 'giraffe'. This distinction, between what we would usually call 'memories' and 'knowledge', is expressed in psychology as a difference between *episodic* and *semantic* memory. Episodic memory is supposed to store events as such, i.e., with some indication of their location, while semantic memory contains representations which are not linked to a particular context.[15]

There is a marked tendency in anthropology to ignore the fact that most representations about traditions are in fact episodic, occasion-bound. This in a sense may be what makes ethnography such a difficult process. There is a systematic discrepancy between what anthropologists are seeking, namely some semantic memory data, and what conversations with informants provide in abundance: memories of singular situations. The link between these two types of representations is not usually described or analysed in anthropological descriptions; when it is mentioned at all, it is only construed as a one-way process, from semantic memory to the interpretation of singular occasions. It is assumed that people use their general representations about the world to organise and understand particular situations. Stated in such vague terms, the hypothesis is beyond doubt. Its extension and generalisation, however, gives rise to what Bloch (1985: 21) calls 'the anthropological theory of cognition', the assumption that the individual process of building representations from singular situations is essentially trivial; it is supposed to consist in the absorption of a ready-made conceptual scheme.

This idea is not only problematical, but plainly inapplicable to traditional contexts. Given the preference for 'event-talk' I have mentioned, and the absence of formal tuition, people *must* build semantic memory data from the limited material presented in a series of singular situations; there is simply nothing else to build on. Therefore the processes through which episodic memories are used to generate knowledge are crucially important to anthropology. Fang people for instance are very rarely told about witchcraft in general terms. In order that they build some representation of what witchcraft is, or the type of actions and effects it involves, they must make use of whatever singular contexts in which the topic is mentioned. People's representations are thus the result of a generalising mechanism, unless we suppose that they are communicated through some magical process.

The 'anthropological theory of cognition' suggests that people have a conceptual scheme, which is used deductively to interpret singular situations; they have certain general ideas about, e.g., witchcraft, and can thus interpret

43

a certain situation as a result of witchcraft. This certainly happens, although it seems strange that anthropology has not studied the opposite process, i.e., people using their memories of singular occasions inductively, to modify the semantic memory and build a representation of the world. The idea that people only make deductions from a 'culture-given' conceptual scheme begs an essential anthropological problem—how people build certain represent-ations of the world from fragments of experience—which in fact must be studied empirically.

My description of evur and other such cultural categories implies that the features of complex cultural constructs, such as a 'system of beliefs' are partly determined by the concrete situations and processes of concept acquisition. The way one learns what evur 'really' means imposes some constraints on the range of possible beliefs about evur; this simple cognitive process is involved in all processes of concept acquisition. When anthropo-logists suppose that beliefs about mana or evur put some constraints on the semantic representation of the notion, they probably put the cart before the horse. People experience situations in which a term is used long before they have any beliefs concerning the corresponding concept. This process is all the more striking with seemingly 'empty' notions; here it is clear that, to a certain extent, the circumstances of acquisition constrain people's beliefs because nothing else is available to limit the extension of these terms. Obviously, there is no theory or abstract principle, which would determine which objects and events are designated; hence people must resort to what is given, namely utterances of different types, and make inferences about the notion from what is conveyed by these utterances and what is implied by the fact that they belong to different registers of discourse.

Conclusions

The hypotheses presented here are of course incomplete, as a description and explanation of traditional categories; this is, in part, because it is difficult to account for the use and representation of categories without explaining many other aspects of traditional interaction, which will be treated in the following chapters. One point in particular deserves special attention. The interaction described here implies that there is a principled division between those discourse registers, on the one hand, which simply use a term in a correct way and convey the common stereotypes about it, and on the other, the registers in which there is supposed to be a description of what the entity designated really is. The distinction may be more simply described in terms of guarantees of truth. Certain types of utterances are supposed to convey some truth about the entities designated; other utterances are not. In the process of building some representation of an entity, the inferences derived from the latter type of utterances are certainly weighed in a specific way. The use of categories in tradition is crucially dependent on this logical division of discourse registers. A study of traditional concepts should therefore describe the processes whereby specific utterances are interpreted as conveying a truth.

3
Criteria of truth

Questions of truth are both crucial to the study of traditions and usually overlooked in anthropological theories. Anthropologists generally avoid using such terms as 'true' and 'false' when describing the status of traditional statements. They use some vague terms, such as 'symbolic' or 'symbolico- expressive', 'significant', 'relevant', 'meaningful', etc. There is a sharp contrast between this usage and the views of the people concerned. No one in a traditional society would ask a diviner to make a 'significant' or 'relevant' statement about any situation, nor would people be satisfied if a shaman claimed to make 'meaningful' findings in his journeys to other worlds. What is sought in such contexts is a *true* description of a situation; indeed, the production of truths is the *raison d'être* of many types of traditional interaction. Divination comes to mind immediately, as a ritual, the explicit purpose of which is to make a true diagnosis; but it is by no means the only such context. All anthropologists have been told by informants that certain persons knew 'the truth' about certain matters because they had been initiated, or that certain myths contained some 'truth' about the ancestors, while other persons or stories were described as mistaken or misleading. Truth is very much a traditional concern, and the anthropological use of woolly terms ('symbolic', 'meaningful', etc.) is rather misleading.

The reason why traditional statements are seldom described as true for the people concerned, in spite of the informants' emphasis on their veracity, is that it seems difficult to apply the terms 'true' and 'false' to such statements without generating a host of difficult problems. The type of things which are said to be 'true' in traditional contexts, and the way people argue for their veracity, do not seem to square with ordinary ideas on truth and falsity. Here are but a few examples of the problems that may arise:

(i) in a traditional context, people sometimes admit the truth of a sentence, without admitting the truth of its paraphrase. They judge a certain utterance 'true', but are doubtful about some direct deduction from the content of the utterance. This is an aspect of the 'literalism' problem mentioned in chapter 1: the words of, e.g., a certain story are said to express a 'truth', but another, logically equivalent formulation is not perceived as conveying a truth;

(ii) in the evaluation of an utterance, the content is sometimes left aside, as it were, and people seem to take into account many other aspects, e.g., the position of the speaker, the circumstances of the utterance, and so on. The limiting case here is that of statements expressed in some ritual language people barely understand, or do not understand at all, yet judge 'true';

(iii) people who say that a given statement is 'true' sometimes do not behave at all in accordance with their alleged conviction. The healer evoked in chapter 2 mentioned ant-hills as an index of witchcraft activities; but people who take this to be true are not especially distressed by the presence of an ant-hill in their backyard, and in any case they would not make too much of such 'hints' in everyday life;

(iv) people seem to take as 'true' many counter-intuitive statements which conflict with what they admit in other contexts, notably in their everyday life. They do not seem at all worried by these apparent contradictions, and this makes it difficult to say that they take both kinds of statements as 'true'.

The list is neither complete nor very sophisticated in its formulation, but it should give an idea of the difficulties encountered. Obviously, these problems are connected; as we will see, most anthropological reflections on the question aim at solving them all in one shot, as it were, by focusing on one of these questions and giving it a simple and plausible solution. In the following pages I will examine some such 'solutions', and show that they are not entirely satisfactory, mainly because the problem itself is not identified precisely enough.

In a first approximation, the problem is that people involved in traditional interaction seem to apply the predicates 'true' and 'false' in a way that would not 'pass muster' in the anthropologist's culture. They apply the predicates to things which, apparently, just cannot be true, and for reasons which do not seem conclusive at all. Now there are three obvious ways of interpreting this, one may assume:

(i) that the people concerned are simply illogical, and do not really have the relevant cognitive equipment;

(ii) that there is a linguistic misunderstanding; the informants either do not really think the statements are 'true' or have a special concept of 'truth' which is adapted to such statements;

(iii) that the odd statements are stored in a special compartment, as it were, so that ordinary criteria do not apply to them.

These three types of interpretation can be found in the anthropological literature, sometimes in combination. The first approach is cited here for the sake of exhaustiveness; extravagant claims about people having no notion of contradiction or logical entailment are not taken seriously or even discussed anymore. The second, 'linguistic' interpretation is implicit in many anthropological descriptions, but it is seldom justified in theoretical terms. Although it should be sufficient on its own, it is often found in combination with the third approach, which constitutes the most widespread interpretation. The idea is that in traditional contexts people have a special way of organising the information conveyed, and more precisely, of relating belief and experience. This is the starting point of most 'theories of belief' in anthropology, which I will examine presently.

Although these approaches are at the centre of well-known, classical controversies, it may be of help to reconsider them in the perspective outlined at the end of chapter 2. Only some discourse registers, i.e., only certain speakers in certain circumstances, are supposed to say the truth about specific topics. Why and how are these speakers, contexts and registers singled out? As we will see, anthropological ideas on truth only provide part of the answer, and some of them provide brilliant solutions for irrelevant questions. Surprisingly, a satisfactory account of traditional 'truth-making' mechanisms will not necessarily focus on the status of 'traditional belief' and on traditional 'conceptions of truth', but on much more limited aspects of cognitive processes. In order to show this, we must briefly examine the limitations of both types of interpretation.

Truth-terms and truth predicates

Let me first consider the idea that different cultures have different 'concepts' of truth. The English terms 'true' and 'false' have a kind of logical transparency or obviousness that cannot always be found in the languages of the societies concerned. In many languages, the terms used to convey the ideas of truth and falsity are not that simple: there can be several terms with different implications, and in most cases the words have other, non-logical meanings. The Fang for instance would make a distinction between *meduk* and *abele*, which could be glossed as 'complicated, intricate, obscure, false' as opposed to 'simple, clear, true'. There is a translation problem here, as the equivalence of such terms and our 'false' and 'true' is not self-evident. The Fang notion seems more complex than an abstract logical predicate; it seems to convey some implicit description of what makes the difference between true and false statements: in the Fang case, there seems to be some connection between a statement being judged 'simple' and its being true. This is by no means exceptional; in most cultures, the words used to describe the truth or falsity of an utterance happen to be conventional

48

metaphors. The most telling example might be the ancient Greek *aletheia*, which could be glossed as 'no-forgetting', 'not-forgettable' or 'attention-demanding'.[1]

A crucial anthropological problem is to account for the strangeness of certain traditional beliefs. Given the apparent absence of strictly logical terms, it is obviously tempting to correlate these two phenomena, and to imagine that people have 'strange' ideas of what is true and what is false because their very *concept* of truth is different from that of the anthropologist. In this account, the associated or metaphorical aspects of the terms considered are in fact central. In his account of Chagga ideas of truth, for example, Gutmann emphasises the links between such related concepts as *lohi*, 'true' and *iloha*, the generic name of sorcery rituals; the implication is that true statements are seen as akin to magical incantations, i.e., binding words (Gutmann 1926: 703, cited by Steiner 1954: 366). We may suppose, in much the same way, that the Fang have a certain complex concept of 'truth-as-simplicity', which cannot be captured by any English word. This idea is what makes the Fang judge as 'true' certain utterances which we would not take in that way. This seems a simple explanation of both the strangeness of the beliefs and the absence of strict Fang equivalents for the English logical terms.[2]

However, the plausibility of this idea vanishes if we examine the linguistic and cognitive processes involved. First let me make a strict distinction between *truth predicates* and *truth-terms*. A truth predicate is an abstract reality, it is a logical term that applies to sentences that say, of what is, that it is, and of what is not, that it is not.[3] A truth-term is a word which (supposedly) expresses the predicate in a certain natural language. Not to confuse logical predicates and natural language terms, let us call the predicate T and −T; we can say that the French *vrai* and *faux* or the Italian *vero* and *falso* are truth-terms used to designate the concepts T and −T, in French and Italian respectively. Now we can rephrase the anthropological idea in more specific terms. The assumption is that the truth-terms of the language can serve as transparent evidence of the type of concepts people possess. If there is no simple term for truth predicates, it means either that people do not possess this type of logical concept at all or that they have a more complex idea of the properties of utterances.

However, both conjectures are highly implausible. Take the example of Fang, in which one finds the terms I glossed as 'simple' and 'complicated'. One could infer from this that the Fang have some idea of simplicity/complicatedness which they use to evaluate people's utterances and come to a conclusion as to their being or not being accurate descriptions of states of affairs. It is not quite clear, however, what kind of intellectual operations this would imply. I am French; if I say I am French, Fang listeners find this abele/'simple'; if I maintain I am Italian, it is meduk/'complicated'. The surface complexity of the utterances is not taken into account; whatever complicated sophistry I use to 'prove' that I am French, people will find the utterances abele/'simple'. So the idea of 'simplicity-truth' cannot be linked to syntactic or rhetorical complexity. It cannot be reduced to the choice of words or phrases either; many formalised traditional statements are very obscure to most Fang people, who nevertheless find them 'simple'. If we carry on, trying to define what 'abele' sentences have in common, we will reach the conclusion that they share no common property at all, except that, for the listeners, they say of what is, that it is and of what is not, that it is not. In short, even if we believe that a strange truth-term expresses something different from truth predicates, we will end up describing this 'something different' as, precisely, the truth predicates. Therefore the hypothesis, that a 'strange' truth-term implies a different concept of truth, seems untenable.

This crude thought-experiment is obviously not all there is to say about the presence of conventional metaphors in truth-terms; as Steiner remarks, the emotional aspects beside the logical use of such terms are obviously crucial for an anthropological account (Steiner 1954: 364). There is a relationship between the metaphor and the logical use of the term, but it does not go in the direction anthropologists would sometimes assume. To return to the Fang example, people say, about utterances that describe non-existent situations, that they are meduk/'complicated'. From the use of the term in such contexts, they can form some idea of what false sentences are typically like: they consist of 'complications' devised by cheaters in order to fool other people. This is consonant with the idea that important false statements do not stem from errors but from conscious attempts to conceal some reality. In any case, what is important here is that such vague ideas are never used as criteria to decide what is true and what is false; rather, they are typical images built from the observation of what has been said to be true and false in the first place.

This is why I used the notion of conventional metaphors in the description of these terms. It is a very common feature of natural languages, that the organisation of certain semantic domains can be described only by using terms derived from another experimental domain. Intellectual arguments, for example, are commonly described in English by using the vocabulary of warfare (a theory is 'attacked', one prepares a 'line of defence', and so on; see Lakoff and Johnson 1977: *passim*, and also Lakoff and Koveceses 1986). In much the same way, anger seems to be described in many languages in terms of a (hot) liquid spilling over a container. Such usages are not literal, but they do not constitute 'live', poetic metaphors either. The use of truth-terms like 'simple' or 'clear' seems to be based on the same type of process. The important point here is that using such conventional phrases does not imply taking their implications literally. People who talk about anger 'pouring over' do not believe they have a small bottle in their hearts which spills over when they run out of patience. In the same way, people can find prototypical true discourse 'clearer' than typical lies, but they do not measure the 'simplicity' of utterances or use it as a criterion of truth.[4]

The mistaken inference from terms to concepts has an immediate appeal, because it seems strange that a language should have no specific word to express such simple predicates as 'true' and 'false'. From this, one is naturally led to suppose that people who express themselves in that language cannot possess the logical truth predicates. But this is a gross mis-representation of the relationship between words, conventional metaphors and cognition.[5] The fact that a concept is not expressed by a single term in the language does not mean that speakers of that language do not possess the concept, and this is clear with regard to colour terms as well as logical terms.[6] The case of truth predicates is by no means exceptional, and many languages lack those meta-linguistic terms which seem so natural to English speakers, like 'word' or 'sentence'. So the strangeness of some traditional truths cannot be explained as an effect of strange concepts of truth.

The logical status of beliefs

To most anthropologists, examining the question of traditional truths necessarily implies dealing with questions of belief. You can explain how certain statements are judged true if you have a good theory of the mechanisms of belief. This idea is so entrenched in the discipline that it takes some explanation to realise that, from a strictly formal point of view, things should go the other way round. Having a set of 'beliefs' (in the anthropological sense of that term) is representing a set of propositions and representing that they are true. Having the belief that ant-hills are an index of witchcraft implies representing (i) that ant-hills are an index of witchcraft and (ii) that the former proposition is true. But no-one can represent *both* without having some idea of what it is for a proposition to be true. So questions of truth are logically more fundamental than questions of commitment or adherence, the usual object of theories of belief. In anthropology, however, things are presented in the other direction. Adherence or commitment is the prime mover, as it were, and truth-ascription one of its consequences. For instance, a witch-doctor says that ant-hills mean witchcraft; people have good reason to trust the speaker; they adhere to the statements he makes; they consequently judge them true. Stated in those vague terms, the proposition is certainly true. In the following pages and chapters I will try to show that it is also extremely ambiguous, and that it is well worth trying to spell out the logical steps in the process of persuasion and adherence. Let me now proceed to anthropological ideas on traditional belief.[7]

The starting point in most theories of belief is the *strangeness* of some exotic beliefs, and the main problem is that of the apparent *irrationality* of people who hold them. How can sensible people really claim, for example, that you can get rid of diseases by reciting some appropriate spell? The question would be easily solved if people were just blatantly illogical or irrational, but they are not, and in their everyday life display a rather cool, rational way of treating problems and evaluating utterances. So the problem is about the processes whereby usual, everyday rationality can be combined with odd claims, especially those made in traditional contexts. This is the most interesting aspect of the old controversy known as 'the rationality debate' (see Wilson ed. 1970, Hollis and Lukes eds. 1982).

Inasmuch as the problem is a cognitive one, a problem of information processing, an obvious solution is to posit that everyday beliefs and traditional claims are not stored or processed in the same way. This is why theories of belief generally focus on the special status of traditional, formal or ritual statements. The distinction can be justified in terms of cognitive salience, although the authors seldom mention that aspect. Ritualised or formalised statements stand out as especially relevant, profound and psychologically salient, and cannot be represented in the same way as those ordinary beliefs which are not really said to be true, simply because everybody takes them for granted. Take for instance two statements made by Fang speakers during my stay:

(a) The sun causes the heat during the day
(b) Ghosts dwell near dark puddles in the forest

Both were held true, so one may think they are both 'beliefs' in the ordinary sense. But the difference is obvious in people's reactions to the denial of such statements. Denying the effects of the sun is denying the obvious, since only small children could be unaware of such facts of life. People always took my denial (rightly) as a joke or a figure of speech. Denying the truth of (b), on the other hand, is a more complex matter. I heard it contested by some Fang speakers, but the audience who had previously judged the statement to be true did not really react much. In fact, stating and denying (b) have one common presupposition, namely that the listeners are invited to represent the speaker as someone who has a specific knowledge of questions of witchcraft and ancestors. I will return to this special feature presently. Suffice it to say that the interpretation of denials, like cognitive salience, memorability, etc., make obvious the distinction between everyday, common-sense beliefs and what is asserted in traditional situations.

The aim of theories of belief is to account for this difference in plausible psychological terms. Having such an account is necessary because many traditional beliefs happen to be incompatible with what is held by common sense. A usual solution is to state that traditional beliefs are stored in a specific box, as it were, and are thus shielded from confrontation with common sense. Their representation, treatment, memorisation involve special mechanisms. An example of such an interpretation is M. Southwold's distinction between 'religious' and 'factual' beliefs (1979: 631ff). Factual beliefs are just beliefs in the ordinary, philosophical sense, i.e., propositions held to be true, without necessarily being represented. Most people can be said to believe that salt is white and water usually liquid, even if it is not explicitly asserted. Moreover, people also have beliefs that have never been represented at all; all my readers believe that Cleopatra did not use a word-processor, although they have never represented it. 'Religious' beliefs on the other hand (which are not necessarily limited to the ordinary extension of the term 'religion') must be represented. If we maintain that the Fang believe in the efficacy of witchcraft, we imply that they do have some explicit representations about witchcraft being efficient, be that a set of general ideas or some memories of specific rituals. Moreover, religious beliefs are often explicitly asserted. So we are not dealing with the same type of processes at all. The reasonings whereby an explicit statement is judged true are not the same as those involved in accepting, e.g., that unsupported objects tend to fall downwards rather than fly in the air.

This is certainly true but insufficient on two accounts. First, there are indefinitely many statements explicitly asserted, which have nothing to do with 'religion', even widely construed. Even if explicit representation is necessary, it is therefore not a sufficient condition for a belief to be treated as 'religious'. We need more specifications. Southwold's idea, however, has one interesting consequence. By insisting on the explicit character of those beliefs as a relevant property, it suggests that what is specific about, e.g., traditional ones may well be the way they are asserted, a point I will examine in the following chapters, from various viewpoints. The second problem with Southwold's distinction is that it does not specify the different processes of, e.g., representation and reasoning, applied to factual and religious beliefs respectively.

This is precisely the starting point of D. Sperber's more sophisticated account of the distinction (1982: 171–7). For Sperber, the main difference involved here is not so much a question of content as one of logical status. Having a belief implies representing a certain sentence, which expresses the 'object' of the belief. It is possible to distinguish between sentences which are simply represented as such (e.g. 'salt is white', 'fishes have no legs') and sentences embedded in a commentary of the form 'it is true that "p"' (e.g. 'it is true that "inflation is bad for the economy"', 'it is true that "ant-hills mean witchcraft"', etc.). *Factual* beliefs are the former and *representational* beliefs the latter type of representations. The point is that most traditional truths are represented in a 'representational' format, e.g., of the form 'the proper interpretation of "p" is true'.

There are some obvious advantages to this proposal, if we consider the

53

problems listed at the beginning of this chapter. For one thing, as Sperber himself points out, a sentence can be embedded in this way without being totally interpreted, and that is precisely what happens, for example, with popular beliefs about specialised subjects like economics: most people would certainly admit that the sentence 'inflation is bad' expresses some truth, without really being able to explain in what way inflation is bad. All they know is that most experts agree on this point, so it must be true; they of course have some vague images as well, about what inflation is like (Sperber: 1982). This may explain how people can assert that a certain statement is true, without feeling committed to its logical consequences. They can admit that 'ant-hills mean witchcraft' is true and not bother to notice ant-hills around them; what they are committed to, in fact, is that some truth is expressed by the proper interpretation of that sentence, although they are not sure what the proper interpretation is (e.g., may *certain* ant-hills mean witchcraft in *certain* contexts? etc.).

Southwold's and Sperber's distinctions make it possible to eliminate some apparent problems with traditional truths. Yet they cannot constitute a general solution, without implying some weird claims about intellectual processes. This in fact is a general defect of the hypotheses proposed in the 'rationality debate' and the main reason why this debate always seems somewhat irrelevant to most anthropologists. The main problem we started with was to explain why and how people find true the statements expressed by certain speakers in certain contexts. This is the basic problem most anthropologists have to solve; its formulation, however, is ambiguous, and I think anthropological theories of belief constantly deal with only one, irrelevant aspect of it. What the 'rationality' hypotheses explain, when they are plausible, is how people can hold certain statements true *and remain reasonable*. That is, people who claim that a ghost can be in two places at once and lift mountains nonetheless lead normal lives, in which they consider that beings have only one location and limited physical capacities. The basic solution is to have the traditional beliefs cordoned off, as it were, so that they do not contaminate everyday cognition. Now, even if these hypotheses are true, they are insufficient to solve another problem, which in fact is the real anthropological one, namely why and how people find these statements true *and not others*.

Anthropological theories have consistently focused on the difference between traditional and *everyday* beliefs. In the account of traditional truths, however, this point is only of marginal interest. What should be described is what makes certain non-everyday beliefs more salient and memorable than others. This is why I have restricted myself to a minimal discussion of the anthropological theories of belief; insofar as their aim is to refine the logical distinctions between various kinds of belief, they are always missing the crucial anthropological problem, and at best provide necessary yet insufficient conditions for traditional statements.

The rationality debate focused on the idea of 'strangeness' on the fact that some people seem convinced by seemingly irrational statements. Therefore many participants in that debate believed that once the problem of strangeness is 'solved', there is nothing more to say about traditional truths. This has the strange implication, that in order to explain why people hold some proposition true, it is enough to show how its refutation is blocked. The rationality debate in its entirety is an illustration of this idea. The recurrent examples are situations like, for example, the Nuer saying that 'twins are birds'. Now the Nuer also *know* that twins are not birds; they cannot fly, they have no feathers and lay no eggs, etc. And the problem is to describe Nuer mental processes in a way that makes it possible to hold both types of belief and stay reasonable. It should be obvious, however, that this still does not explain why Nuer people believed twins to be birds in the first place. What makes the idea of birdlike twins so salient?

Pushed to their logical consequences, theories of belief would suggest that twins are said to be birdlike simply because (i) 'that's the tradition' and (ii) the idea is shielded from empirical refutation. In other words, people are given a catalogue of beliefs with no intrinsic justification, and whose refutation happens to be blocked. They therefore believe them. This of course does not hold. There are indefinitely many beliefs, whose refutation is blocked or impossible, and which no-one pays any attention to. Furthermore, there are indefinitely many beliefs in the current repertoire of any human group, which will be forgotten, left aside or transformed. Some statements, however, will become psychologically salient, will be memorised and repeated in subsequent occurrences. Why are they treated differently? This is a crucial question for the study of tradition, a question about which theories of belief have nothing to say.

Conceptions and criteria

Obviously, the strategies examined here do not provide a satisfactory account of the problems of traditional truths. The approach which considers the logical status or the overall organisation of beliefs describes only part of the cognitive processes involved; it does not account for the particular salience of traditional truths. The interpretation, which stresses the influence of linguistic factors, generates some untenable hypotheses unless it is substantially qualified. In fact both approaches have a common defect, in that they are far too general to give any empirically significant explanation of traditional truths.

In both conceptions it is taken for granted that the problem requires a general solution. The way statements are judged true in traditional contexts can be explained by resorting to general hypotheses, about the way propositions are stored or the type of logical predicates available in the language. The problem with such solutions is that they are always either too weak or too powerful. Theories of belief, for instance, when they are plausible, are much too powerful. They suggest that people, if given an explicit catalogue of statements with blocked refutation or 'representational' status, will believe them all. This is obviously untrue, and the theory is not fine-grained enough in its description to account for the fact that only some such statements are actually believed and memorised. The linguistic analysis on the other hand is much too weak, in the sense that if it were true, if people really had complex concepts irreducible to truth predicates, it would be very difficult for them to hold true even the most pedestrian everyday statements.

The reason why these interpretations are unsatisfactory is that they are directed at the wrong kind of intellectual objects. Here I must emphasise the difference between conceptions and criteria of truth. Conceptions of truth, in a general sense, can be described as sets of general propositions about the relationships between sentences and states of affairs in general, or about the meaning of truth-terms. The interpretations described here are entirely about the conceptions of truth implicit in traditional statements, and they are based on two assumptions, namely that when people judge a given utterance true, they are implicitly, perhaps unconsciously, applying certain abstract principles about language and reality to the case at hand, and that the principles applied in traditional contexts are different from those obtaining in other cultures or contexts.

An extreme form of this idea is M. Hollis's hypothesis, that in ritual contexts people abandon their usual conception of truth as correspondence (what is true is what describes the world the way it really is) to adopt a 'coherentist' view (statements are true if they 'fit' in what one already knows about the world) (Hollis 1970: 223). Now this is unsatisfactory, not only for empirical reasons (people sometimes find true ritual statements which contradict what they usually admit), but also in principle; I will argue that the difference between the veracity of traditional, ritualised statements, and that of ordinary discourse, just cannot be a question of conceptions of truth and therefore has to be explained by specific criteria of truth.

The fact that conceptions of truth, in whatever form, will give no satisfactory answer, should be clear from the fact that such explanations, as I said above, are always either too strong or too weak. Hollis's hypothesis is no exception; if you admit that traditional statements are judged on their coherence with other beliefs, then you make it possible for people to entertain indefinitely many beliefs, which in fact they would never hold. This recurrent problem is in fact the consequence of a logical mistake. It is probably true that any specific truth-ascription implies some conception of truth; but it would be wrong to assume that the converse is true, namely that a conception of truth implies specific truth-ascriptions, or in other words that specific truth-ascriptions can be deduced from a conception of truth. This is clearly false. People do not judge statements on the sole basis of their (unconscious) theory of truth, they have many other reasons for finding specific statements true or false. This is where criteria of truth become pertinent.

Criteria of trugh are *specific* reasons for finding an utterance true. They concern the content of the utterance, its relationship to other propositions held to be true, the person of the speaker, an evaluation of his or her knowledge, and so on. They cannot be generated by abstract principles, they are grounded in specific descriptions of the utterances concerned. The Fang judgement, for instance, which decides it is true that ant-hills are signs of witchcraft, is not the result of a transcendental deduction or of a special use of the term 'true'. Fang listeners take the statement to be true because they know this specific speaker is reliable, has been initiated into anti-witchcraft rituals. Criteria are diverse and can be conflicting. Take for instance the statement 'there are three sexes in giraffes' uttered by a reputable biologist; in such a case, the evaluation of the speaker and of the content may be conflicting for a listener with a poor knowledge of biology. It is a well-known fact of life that the judgement on many statements is thus suspended, either because the evidence is lacking or because it is conflicting.

Criteria and criteria types

Obviously, if we want to explain why people hold true certain statements and not others, we will need to examine their criteria of truth. If we want to understand why certain speakers in certain contexts are supposed to speak the truth, we must study the criteria applied to those precise contexts and speakers. The reason why this is not recognised in theories of traditional truth is that the task seems impossible; since criteria are specific, concern the specific speaker and context, they must be as many as the contexts studied. The criteria applied to Fang diviners will not be the same as those relevant for Shilluk priests or Zande witch-doctors. Therefore the study of criteria is a question of ethnographic description, not anthropological theory. Nothing general can be said about them.

This is not entirely true. Criteria are indeed specific, but this does not preclude them from being classified in a few general *types*. If, for example, some people hold true whatever is said by reputed physicists, reputed biologists and reputed sociologists, it is likely that the criteria applied to different contexts belong to a single criteria type, to do with reputed scientists. It must be possible to establish a taxonomy of criteria of truth. If we assume that traditional truths are special in some way, we will try to describe the common features of the criteria applied to traditional statements; in other words, our taxonomy will have a special node labelled 'traditional criteria type', maybe with a few appropriate sub-types, to distinguish between different kinds of traditional contexts, as the case may be.

It is therefore conceivable that there is a common criteria type for traditional contexts in general. In fact, the 'common' anthropological conception of tradition includes a hypothesis about that criteria type. Unfortunately, it is a very poor hypothesis. Its main theme is what could be called the principle of authority. We know that in traditional contexts truth is reserved to specific speakers and specific circumstances. The principle of authority says that there is no mystery at all in this process; in a traditional context, whatever is said by certain people or whatever is said in the context of certain ritual operations is true. The Fang believe that ant-hills are an index of witchcraft because it is said by a witch-doctor during the appropriate ritual. The criterion of truth is that whatever witch-doctors say is true; if we add that whatever the elders and the ancestor cult specialists say is true, we have a fairly complete list of Fang criteria. As for the general criteria type, it could be formulated like this: whatever is said by persons who hold some knowledge bequeathed by former generations is true.

It is important here not to be confused about who is making the hypothesis. We suppose that people involved in traditional interaction, when they evaluate the statements made in specific contexts, represent those statements as the consequence of a 'competence' that is transmitted from generation to generation. The common conception suggests that this is in the head of the people concerned. As we saw in chapter 1, the common conception also implies that this is the real state of affairs, that there is a real competence and a real transmission. These are two different hypotheses, one is about the way people interpret some utterances, the other about what really happens. In chapter 1, I presented various arguments against the idea that things really happen that way, against the idea of a real transmission of world views. Even if my arguments were right, it might remain that the 'transmission of competence' is the interpretation made by the actors involved in such situations. That is what we want to examine now. Is this idea of traditional 'authority' really implied by people's reasoning about traditional utterances?

As a description of people's reasoning, the 'principle of authority' is obviously unsatisfactory. It has some *prima facie* evidence; people do say things like 'this is true because the initiates say it'. The principle, however, is insufficient and question-begging. It is insufficient, in the sense that every anthropologist has met sceptics and dissenters, and a description of traditional criteria should account for such cases, which become incomprehensible if established competence is all there is about traditional truth. Moreover, the hypothesis is question-begging. It assumes that people find true, for instance, whatever is said by ritual specialists. But these specialists are recognised as legitimate, because they have certain characteristics which make them 'truthful'. To return to my Fang example, the witch-doctor's utterance (about ant-hills as indices of witchcraft) is judged true because the speaker is an evur-bearer, has performed the evur-shaping rituals, has undergone a specific initiation comprising some direct dealings with ghosts, and so on. That Fang listeners find his utterances true 'because he is an established witch-doctor' is right only as a shorthand version of the interaction. But in the process of shortening it we have left aside the crucial reasonings which are relevant to truth-ascription. In all logic, truth here is not a function of a social position, but a consequence of the specific representations people have about the processes leading to the position.

The same argument applies, *mutatis mutandis*, to contexts instead of positions. It is sometimes stated that the participants in traditional ritual find true whatever is said by possessed people. Again, this is just shorthand. The criterion of truth is not that possession implies truth, but that possession is represented in such a way that it is likely to result in the production of true utterances. If you use the shorthand version and forget that it is just shorthand, then you have the 'principle of authority', saying that whatever is said in proper ritual contexts is true. But that does not hold as a description of the participants' reasonings.

All this may seem obvious. Indeed, it is obvious, and ethnographic descriptions of *particular* traditional situations always give the 'longhand' version of the reasonings involved. They give all the relevant specific representations which make witch-doctors or possession truthful. In anthropological theories, however, we only find the shorthand idea that traditional truths are judged true because of the authority of position and context. This happens because the longhand reasonings I have mentioned are supposed to be specific to each culture and context, and to have nothing much in common except, precisely, the idea of authoritative social positions and favourable contexts. The Fang reasonings about witch-doctors and the Zande reasonings about diviners are supposed to be totally different, the only common idea being that authority is vested in specific positions and operations.

In the following chapters I will try to show that this is entirely wrong. The criteria of truth and the reasoning applied to Fang witchcraft, Zande divination, or Malagasy ritual discourse are indeed specific, but they share important, non-trivial characteristics beyond the mere identification of specific positions and operations. The 'criteria type' applied to traditional interaction can be described in some detail, avoiding the question-begging claims usually found in anthropological theories.

Criteria and situations

As I said at the beginning of this chapter, traditional truths seem problematic; in a traditional context, people do not seem to judge utterances in the same way as in everyday conversation. The object of judgement seems different, since people can assert that a statement is true and be doubtful about its implications. Also, the grounds for judgement are puzzling, in that the

59

content of the utterances is often left aside. But anthropological reflections on truth do not have any satisfactory explanations to put forward. Instead, they focus on questions like rationality and the status of belief, which are for the most part irrelevant to the problem at hand. Such theories only provide a general framework in which it is not entirely unreasonable to hold traditional 'beliefs'. This, obviously, is insufficient and does not even begin to explain for what reasons people hold these beliefs. It is impossible to account for traditional truths in a satisfactory way without focusing on the type of criteria used. Against a common anthropological assumption, I have argued that it is in fact possible to find common properties, specific to traditional interaction, in the reasoning whereby statements produced in various cultures and contexts are judged true.

In the description of abstract conceptions of truth, the characteristics of traditional truths mentioned at the beginning of this chapter pose difficult problems. In the description of the specific criteria of truth on the other hand, these characteristics are of great help. They are common features of the truths produced in traditional contexts, and therefore constitute an excellent starting point for our inquiry. In the following chapters I will therefore focus on what may seem the most puzzling characteristic, namely that traditional truths are asserted in particular situations, which require a combination of specific actions and specific actors to perform them. Furthermore, the expression of truths makes it necessary to take many ritual precautions. Diviners for instance must avoid certain foods or activities, ritual specialists 'prepare' themselves. 'Precautions' or 'preparations' concern both the utterances and the persons. Special forms of speech and discourse registers are used in traditional contexts. An utterance takes on a special value, by virtue of the actions or technical operations by which it has been produced, e.g., a divination procedure, or by virtue of the special language, or vocabulary, which is used. The precautions can also focus on the very person of the speaker. Not all speakers are in the same position as regards specific domains of reality, not all of them are in a position that allows them to utter true statements. In most cases such a position is the consequence of a specific initiation, either a 'tribal' rite everyone has to undergo or a more specialised initiation, such as the Fang witch-doctors' apprenticeship mentioned in chapter 2.

Although such precautions are always mentioned in ethnographic studies, they are supposed to be part of those contextual factors which provide the setting, as it were, whereas the content of the utterances is essential. This description, however, is misleading; to the people concerned, these precautions are essential ingredients in the production of truths. Traditional statements are judged true because they come from 'customised' persons, as it were, and require 'customised' speech. In order to describe the type of criteria of truth applied to the traditional statements, we must therefore examine both types of customisation.

4

Customized speech (I): truth without intentions

In many or most cultures, divination is considered a reliable source of true statements about important events or states of affairs. In traditional contexts it constitutes a crucial 'truth – making' procedure. Anthropological theories, however, do not say much about the intellectual processes whereby divinatory statements are judged true. Although there is a number of precise, sometimes illuminating hypotheses about the social contexts of divination and 'divination-driven' decisions, the cognitive aspects of the phenomenon are relatively neglected. In this chapter I will try to put forward some hypotheses about the cognitive mechanisms which make divinatory procedures and the observation of omens a plausible source of truth.

Anthropological arguments: a school of red herrings

Before examining some general properties of divination procedures, let me first focus on some common anthropological ways of avoiding the question of veracity. They constitute a vague pre-theoretical picture of divination, which interferes with the anthropological description but cannot be taken as a serious theoretical attempt. The common picture usually implies some general claims about traditional statements, like the fact that divinatory truth is a function of authoritative positions, or that the statements made in divination are not supposed to be 'true', but simply 'relevant' or 'meaningful' (see chapter 3). While the idea of truth reduced to 'meaningful' statements is simply untenable given the ethnographic data, the 'principle of authority', taken as an explanation of truth criteria, just begs the question. Some claims, however, concern the specific features of divinatory truth; they can be summarised as follows:

1 The divinatory statement is manipulated. This is one of the commonest arguments. It runs as follows: although diviners try to convince their customers that they are just communicating the results generated by a neutral procedure, they actually manipulate the diagnosis, typically by using background knowledge about the situation at hand, the clients' wishes and the likely outcomes of present states of affairs.

2 The content of the statement makes it irrefutable. The idea is that divinatory statements are expressed in such an ambiguous way that any subsequent course of events would confirm them. A paradigmatic case is the Pythic oracle predicting the demise of a great empire, without saying precisely which. Mendonsa opens his account of Sisala divination with the statement that 'the viability of divination rests on the fact that a divinatory pronouncement can never be proved wrong' (Mendonsa 1982: 109). This is sometimes used in conjunction with the previous argument, although either of them, alone, should provide a sufficient explanation.

3 Refutation is blocked by 'secondary elaboration'. This phenomenon, brilliantly described in Evans-Pritchard's study of Zande oracles (1937) is familiar to all anthropologists: the empirical refutation of a particular divinatory diagnosis only casts doubt on that particular ritual, not on the divinatory technique in general. People find special reasons to explain away a particular failure, by assuming, e.g., that the diviner had eaten forbidden foods or that the particular ritual was not properly performed, so that they carry on relying on divination and oracles in general.

These claims can be found in various combinations, either explicit or implicit, in many anthropological monographs and theoretical essays. Whatever the presentation, they do not constitute a satisfactory account of the veracity of divination. Each of the arguments is insufficient, in that many counter-examples can be found, so that they are often used together in *ad hoc* combinations. In order to go beyond this composite, and vaguely inconsistent view of divination, it may be of help to examine the flaws of each argument.

It is somewhat ironical, that anthropologists dealing with the veracity of divination manage to avoid the question by resorting to the standard arguments of enemies of divination or omens. Thus, the idea of a manipulation of diagnosis, based on background knowledge, can be found in many pre-anthropological writings. The idea that diviners try to keep their customers happy, by telling them what they want to hear, can be found in Cicero's *De Divinatione*. The idea of background knowledge as the real basis of relevant diagnoses is so pervasive in the anthropological literature that it contaminates outsiders. K. Thomas for instance states, in his account of classical magic and religion, that English 'diviners...like their African counterparts, maintained their prestige by a combination of fraud and good psychology' (1971: 289, see also 50ff.). This argument is clearly insufficient. Not all divination rituals make such manipulation possible; on the contrary, many procedures are organised as series of yes/no questions which leave no interpretative leeway to the diviner. Moreover, if diviners were experts at making judicious statements, the problem of empirical refutation should never arise. But it does arise, so the argument is at best insufficient, and in any case would not explain why the procedure should be taken as an indispensable element.

The second argument is based on the alleged difficulty of refuting divinatory statements, because of their intrinsic vagueness. Again, this anthropological hypothesis about divination is the modern version of a classical argument against divination.[1] The argument is based on the hypothesis that, in certain circumstances, subjects hold a statement true just because its refutation is blocked. This, as I pointed out in chapter 3, is obviously insufficient, and certainly does not explain why a statement is considered plausible in the first place. In any culture, there are many contexts where people make claims whose form or content puts them beyond refutation. Not all such claims are considered convincing, so that a description of divination simply cannot avoid the question, of why divination should be convincing. Moreover, many divinatory statements are specific and predictive enough to be refuted by subsequent events. This is where the 'secondary elaboration' argument comes into play. This idea, although very popular with anthropologists, is not really satisfactory either. True, people do resort to such reasonings to protect the basic tenets of their beliefs, including their faith in divination, but we are left again with the crucial question, why should it be protected in the first place? There must be some reasons why divination procedures appear convincing, and therefore worth protecting, which the notion of 'secondary elaboration' does not explain.

To summarise, these statements about divination just beg the crucial question of the veracity of divinatory diagnoses.[2] Moreover, this common (implicit) conception goes against what the clients themselves say about divination. The diviners' clients consider that the statements are true because they have been generated by the technique. They must have some representations which make it plausible that utterances brought about in this way are true. While they insist that a divinatory statement is different from ordinary discourse, in that it is more certainly true, the anthropological conception implies that this difference is just a matter of decorum or cunning. If this is the case, the universal existence of divinatory procedures is inexplicable. In the following pages I will try to show that it is possible to put forward a theory of divination that goes beyond these question-begging ideas.

Elements and types of divination

Divination rituals are supposed to generate true statements. This implies that the participants in the rituals must represent a specific criterion of truth, which applies to statements generated in this way. Anthropological models tend to suggest that the veracity of divination is just a 'cultural axiom', which is admitted without any justification, but this is an ambiguous claim. True, people who participate in divination rituals seldom bother to elaborate an abstract and explicit 'theory' of divination and truth. But most criteria of truth are implicit, in everyday life as well as in science or tradition. As I mentioned in chapter 3, criteria of truth are not necessarily generated by abstract theories of language and reality; they are specific empirical hypotheses, which concern a certain domain of reality, certain ways of making statements and inferences, and so on. These hypotheses must focus on three main elements:

(i) the *situation*, i.e., the undefined state of affairs which is supposed to be the cause of the problem at hand. People who consult a diviner must have the idea that there is 'something the matter'. In a domain to which they have little or no access, there is a definite state of affairs which has effects in their lives. Although people generally have no specific representation of what that state of affairs is, or only have conjectures (otherwise they would not need a diviner), they know that the state of affairs exists and has some effects;

(ii) the *procedure*, the set of operations which make divinatory situations different from ordinary situations of communication. It is important to note here, against the widespread ideas mentioned above, that the procedures involved are always taken as what actually *produce* the statements. The inspired mediums attribute the message they communicate to some external entity; the statements would not have been the same if they had not been possessed or otherwise influenced by that entity. In the same way, the result of a technical operation, e.g., shaking dice, is conceived as the foundation of the divinatory statements.

(iii) the *diagnosis*, i.e., the description of the 'situation' at hand, which is achieved through the use of the procedure.[3]

Actors cannot participate in divination rituals without entertaining some representations about these three elements and their combination. In what follows I will argue that if the elements are represented as having certain specific connections, then the situation as a whole can be considered more likely to generate true statements than other discourse situations. In order to show this, we must examine some (non question-begging) anthropological ideas on people's representations of the divinatory activity. I will focus on two fundamental ideas which can be found in anthropological sources, sometimes in combination. Both contain a grain of truth and point at some important aspects of the rituals; unfortunately, we will see that they are not sufficient as a description of the criterion of truth used by clients in the interpretation of divination.

Before describing these models, however, it is necessary to give a brief survey of the types of institutions to which they are supposed to apply. The term 'divination' covers various types of rituals; and the anthropological models are generally inspired by divinatory procedures of a given type, thus neglecting some obvious features of the other types. To give but a brief survey of the varieties of divination, we must distinguish between two broad types of procedures, and also contrast these 'technical' forms of divination with the observation of omens and portents.

First, most authors agree on a distinction between two types of divination founded on the type of technique used. Divination can be performed, either by putting a specialist in an appropriate state of 'inspiration' (notably in cases of possession), or by using specific instruments: cards, cowries, dice, sacrificed animals, etc. In the latter case the interpretation of mantic signs can be given in advance, as e.g., in the Mesopotamian 'catalogues' which list thousands of omens and portents and their interpretation. The distinction between 'inspired' and 'constrained' divinations is always present in the anthropological literature, although the exact terms may vary: Reynolds (1963: 118) calls them 'mental' and 'mechanical', and Bottero (1987: 58) 'inspired' versus 'deductive' procedures. There is in fact a continuum between totally constrained techniques in which the interpretative work is ready-made, as it were, and pure cases of possession. Variably 'constrained' types of divination, with different purposes and cognitive effects, can coexist in certain cultures (see Bauer and Hinnant 1980: *passim*). Like most analytical distinctions used in anthropology, this one refers more to ideal types than to real differences, and most cases fall somewhere between these types, as Zeitlyn points out (1987: 5ff.).

Another distinction is commonly made, between divination as a technical operation and the observation of natural omens. The latter are special in that they are available in the natural environment; they do not require any intentional manipulation. While dice are thrown and cards drawn from a pack, the flight of birds, the shapes of clouds and other such portents are not brought about by a human agent.[4] Again, however, the contrast holds only between ideal types; in actual rituals there is a considerable overlap between omens and divinatory signs. The decision to select certain phenomena, or certain aspects of these, as ominous, e.g., the flight of certain birds at a certain time, is clearly close to a technical operation which can only generate certain formal combinations.

However blurred in actual ritual practice, these distinctions are relevant in that they provide the starting point for anthropological interpretations of the clients' expectations and intellectual processes as regards the divinatory diagnoses. Here I will mainly focus on two types of interpretation, which I will call 'intentional' and 'semiotic' respectively.

Divination, messages and 'hidden' speakers

In a widespread interpretation, divination is described as a ritual aimed at making explicit some messages coming from ancestors, gods or spirits. This is how Loewe and Blacker define it, at the beginning of their collection on divination in 'great traditions' (1981: 4). The description seems natural enough in cases of 'inspired' or 'emotive' divination, close to possession, and it is no surprise to find it explicitly defended in ancient sources. After all, the prototypical Pythic oracles were primarily conceived as indirect messages from the god.[5] 'Inspired' divination is generally described as a ritual whose aim is to receive explanations or orders from transcendent entities. Even in cases of 'constrained' or 'mechanical' procedures, this description is often close to the accounts given by the participants. In the extremely varied African systems it is common to interpret the diviner's task as one of translation; the bush-spirits or the ancestors are supposed to 'talk' through geomantic patterns or the behaviour of oracular chickens. This particular interpretation has influenced anthropologists mainly because it is what the practitioners often express, when they try to rationalise or justify their practice.

This interpretation, however, is not altogether satisfactory, because it relies on an ambiguous description. I would argue that the 'intentional' model points at important properties of the divination contexts but misinterprets them. In order to understand these features, it is necessary to leave aside, for a while, the alleged communication with transcendent entities and focus on the actual communication situation that is set up during a divinatory seance. Obviously, making a diagnosis through a divinatory procedure is not equivalent to making a common assertion. According to Zempleni (1986: *passim*), it should be seen as a special type of 'speech act', in which a specific action is supposed to result in and guarantee an utterance, in that case an assertion; what a theory should describe is the formal conditions of this original speech act. Divination is a form of communication between diviner and clients in which the pragmatic aspects of common assertions are modified. In normal conversation, literal assertions are interpreted as implying that the speaker is commited to the truth of what is expressed by the sentence; asserting 'giraffes live in Africa' implies being committed to this idea of their location. In divinatory utterances, however, there seems to be a dissociation between the person who actually makes the statement (the diviner) and the person(s) or agencies responsible for the statement. The diviners speak, yet it is not they who are committed to the truth of their words (Zempleni 1986). Among the Tallensi, for instance, the diviner and the consulter hold a wand and move it above a divinatory material consisting of several stones. The answer to each specific question is given by the direction the sticks point to. As Fortes points out, the Tallensi 'insist that neither the consulter nor the diviner knows what is going to be the outcome of the divination session. They insist that it is the ancestors who move the stick and put the words in their mouth' (Fortes 1966: 419).

This is a very general property of divinations. Diviners take great pains to convince their clients that their own representation of the situation concerned is immaterial, and that their task is to translate what comes up in the stone patterns or the aspect of the entrails; in the same way, they commonly attribute their mistakes to the ancestors or spirits, who are said to have lied to the expert or deceived him. Now, if the diviner himself is not taken as the one who originates the message, then it seems plausible to surmise that the message is attributed to other, transcendent speakers, e.g., gods, spirits or ancestors. All this seems to suggest that the 'intentional' interpretation is right, and that the participants do represent a 'hidden speaker' as the origin of the diagnosis.

This, however, is where the mistake lies. By putting the actual, human speaker between brackets, as it were, the ritual does not necessarily imply that another, hidden speaker is represented. In many societies, divinatory statements can be generated in the absence of definite hypotheses about their origin. Some forms of divination dispense with the idea of 'another world' or 'other entities' altogether. To give but one example, French Bocage witchcraft, as described in Favret-Saada's monograph (1980), is anything but intellectually fanciful. There are no refined cosmological ideas, no complex notion of the various 'forces' involved, no theory of how witches manage to bring about their victim's demise. The victims are just faced with an inexplicable succession of untoward events, until some well-wisher suggests that recurrent misfortune cannot be attributed to bad luck, that there must be 'something more' to the situation. The experts involved in the identification of the problem and the unbewitching rituals base their diagnoses on a fairly common interpretation of the series of cards drawn from a pack (Favret-Saada and Contreras 1984), which makes it possible both to identify the problem as a witchcraft situation and to give some indications as to the identity of the witch. The diviners are eager to convince their clients that their technique involves no 'mystical' aspect at all: the diagnosis is 'just there', transparently expressed by the succession of cards drawn. Neither the clients nor the diviners ever wonder through what process or agency a conflicting human situation can be thus revealed by a pack of cards. There is no mention of any mediating entity, and no-one seems interested in pursuing the idea. Obviously, such intellectual concerns pale into insignificance, when compared with the strong emotive aspects of the situation; for witchcraft is always conceived as a matter of life and death. During the long series of unbewitching rituals that follow, the same principle holds; clients just 'observe' that certain rituals work and others do not, and that's that.

The 'intentional' paradigm is therefore insufficient. Diviners seem eager to dismiss the idea that the diagnoses could depend upon their own intentions. Dismissing this, however, does not necessarily make room, as it were, for another, imaginary speaker. In spite of this error, the 'intentional' model will allow us to go further in the description of the discourse situation. It implies that the connection between situation, procedure and diagnosis, as represented by the participants, excludes the mediation of the actual speaker's communicative intentions. In the following section I will turn to another interpretation, which is related to this idea and suggests that the actors represent some form of direct connection between situation and diagnosis.

Signs and diagnosis: semiotic links

In the semiotic understanding of divination, people who consult diviners, and diviners themselves, are supposed to conceive of their activity as the observation and deciphering of signs. In this conception, the signs are either natural, in the case of omens and portents, or artificial, i.e., produced by a divinatory technique, and they stand for the actual state of affairs the client wants to know about. The divinatory activity consists in deciphering the correct meaning to these signs, and the relationship between signifiers (divinatory elements) and signifieds may be more or less constrained, according to the particular features of the system considered.

Not surprisingly, this hypothesis is often based on the idea that the religious activity of diviners, on the one hand, and the more pedestrian capacity of predicting natural occurrences on the other are just varieties of the same interpretive process. Divination is conceived of as an extension, to transcendent domains, of the ordinary observation of coincidences or conjunctions in natural phenomena. A good example of this reasoning is Quintus's defense of divination, in the first part of Cicero's *De Divinatione*. According to Quintus, the prediction of future occurrences is in fact a very ordinary activity, a skill derived from the accumulation of observation. Experienced sailors can predict the occurrence of a storm from the observation of clouds, winds and waves. In an even more pedestrian way, everyone can predict from the shape of a seed, what the shape of the grown plant will be like. Divination, at least in some of its practices, is just an extension of this activity (*Div*. I.vii.12ff.).

The idea that diviners and clients are involved in the deciphering of natural or artificial 'signs' for unobservable situations, seems convincing for several reasons. First of all, it is the natural idiom of many forms of inductive divination, and seems to give a good account of the fact that divinatory signs are often grouped in a system. In all systems of 'mechanical' divination, the mantic material consists of randomising procedures that give certain structured answers. For instance, the geomantic signs are grouped in established patterns, which combine in larger patterns, and so on. This type of syntactic organisation makes them look very much like any abstract 'language' generated by simple rules, and this I suppose is why many authors find the analogy with other semiotic systems illuminating.[6]

There are some limitations, however, to this semiotic interpretation. First, while it seems to fit cases of constrained or mechanical divination, it is a rather inadequate interpretation of inspired divination. Divinatory diagnoses which are given in the context of trance or possession do not usually display a system of formal signs. Also, and more importantly, the idea of signs is extremely ambiguous, and just begs the question of the fundamental relationship established between some state of affairs the clients want to know about, and the diagnoses themselves. In order to show why this is important, we must return to very general properties of divination ritual.

The semiotic model does not describe the link between the situation and the diagnosis in a satisfactory way. The idea that people represent the diagnosis as a series of 'signs' is either trivial or false. It may be taken to imply that the participants represent the relationship between diagnosis and situation as a relationship between signs and their referent. In this interpretation, the idea is trivially true. The diagnosis, after all, is supposed to be a description of the situation at hand. But giving a description of something always consists in producing some signs or tokens that stand for the thing described. If, on the other hand, the semiotic interpretation suggests that divination provides a systematic equivalence between certain semiotic features and their interpretation, so that there is a cultural divinatory code, then it is clearly false in most cases. True, some societies have developed such catalogues of divinatory signs and portents; but this is not universal, far from it.[7]

The model therefore cannot solve the question at hand, namely why the 'signs' produced by divinatory procedures are supposed to be more reliable than other, ordinary 'signs'. As we will see in the next sections, there is an important truth in the idea that the solution (the identification of the criterion of truth) lies in people's representations of the link between situation and diagnosis. The merit of the semiotic interpretation is that it lays stress on the fact that this link is represented as a *direct* connection; as it stands, however, the interpretation is not sufficiently accurate and general.

To sum up, both general ideas on the actors' representations seem insufficient. Both models rely on the idea that divination rituals are represented as communication procedures. As I will now try to show, there are some limitations to this idea, which cannot really explain the intellectual mechanisms whereby divination is judged truthful. This question can be solved only if we have a precise description of the connection established, in the participants' minds, between a certain state of affairs and its divinatory description.

Guarantees of veracity

It may be of help here to focus on the specific guarantees of truth which are given by divinatory procedures and on the factors that may disrupt the ritual. In what follows I will examine some examples, and try to outline a description of divination which takes such aspects into account.

The first example is a fairly straightforward case of 'constrained' or 'mechanical' procedure, taken from the description of the Mundang system of divination by A. Zempléni and A. Adler (1972). The Mundang consult the diviners in order to find out the position of the *cox sinri* (earth-spirits) and *mozumri* (ancestors) as regards crucial questions, notably about political matters. This is made manifest through the patterns formed by stones thrown down on the ground. These patterns are themselves integrated into larger stereotypical combinations, which give definite yes/no answers to the client's questions. The different aspects of the client's situation are represented by several circles of stones in front of the diviner. The stones stand for the parts of the client's body, the members of his or her family and household, the walls of the house, the hours of the day, the seasons, and so on. The divinatory session consists of a long series of 'deals', each of which is supposed to describe the state of one of these elements. More than a hundred specific questions are thus given a definite positive or negative answer, and the combination of all these minute diagnoses constitutes the divinatory description of the situation at hand.

The order of the questions on the check-list never changes; the first four 'deals' are crucial, since they concern the 'state of veracity' of the divinatory session itself. If the results are positive, then the session as a whole is going to yield a true description of the situation; when they are negative, the diviner 'shuffles' the stones and deals again, or decides to bring the session to an end. The results of the first four deals guarantee the truth of what is to follow. As Zempléni and Adler remark, 'the diviner is given an opportunity to cast doubt upon his own activity...The statements can be biased by the very ancestors and spirits whose intentions are being examined' (1972: 100, my translation). In other words, the Mundang rituals state, not only that the situation is such and such, but also that the description itself is reliable.

The possibility of checking divination by another divination is in fact widespread, if not universal. We can find a similar procedure in the traditional divination of the Sisala of Northern Ghana (Mendonsa 1982). The diviner (*vugura*) is typically consulted before and after funerals, first to make sure that none of the mourners had been involved in witchcraft rituals against the deceased, then to find out what the actual cause of death was. But diviners are also consulted about all kinds of important matters, notably about relationships with the ancestors. Divination gives access to the hidden world called *fafa*; it is 'the only legitimate mechanism whereby the Sisala can receive feed-back from the ancestors' (Mendonsa 1982: 191). The Sisala readily admit that divination is not altogether reliable. The fallibility of the procedures is attributed to several causes. Diviners may just invent stories to please their client; also, the ancestors may be angry with a diviner and make him lose his ability; and it is generally accepted that not all diviners are equally insightful (Mendonsa 1982: 190; see also Mendonsa 1976).

An institutional procedure, called *dachevung*, makes it possible to verify divinatory statements. Whenever a client wants to check the veracity of a diviner's assertions, he goes to another diviner and asks for a *dachevung*. This is a shortened version of the traditional ritual. The client draws several marks in the dust, some of which stand for the first diviner's assertions. The new diviner, who is not told the meaning of the marks, points his stick towards some of them. If he happens to choose the 'right' marks, those which stand for the diviner's statements, then these statements are confirmed.

Similar phenomena are reported by Fortes among the Tallensi, and by Zeitlyn in his study of Mambila divination in Cameroon. The Tallensi conceive the failure of divinatory diagnoses as caused by the ancestors. At the beginning of the sessions there is a small ordeal to decide whether the ancestors are willing to talk. In one such case observed by Fortes, the ancestors are against talking because the diviner has not made the sacrifice they wanted (1966: 418). A similar point can be made about the Cameroonian Mambila spider divination, as described by Zeitlyn (1988). The technique involves a spider, which is left under an upturned pot. Trying to escape, the spider moves a series of divinatory 'cards' or leaves, whose subsequent positions give a yes/no answer to the question put by the diviner. Zeitlyn reports that 'the pots may also be asked whether any witchcraft is attempting to interfere with them' (1988: 13).

There seems to be a circular aspect to these divinatory checks on divination, which consist in evaluating a procedure by resorting to that same procedure. This however does not seem to bother either clients or diviners. As Zeitlyn points out, 'this is the only place where a Western logician can quarrel with their practice, but I did not succeed in pointing out the fallacy.... No one I spoke to saw the problem as I did' (1988).

These examples are complex cases of 'mechanical' divination. Part of the complication comes from the apparent circularity of the guarantee. One should not, however, be blinded by the circularity to such an extent that one does not notice the important property of divinatory diagnoses that it illustrates. Here I will try to show that such examples are remarkable, not because of the circularity, but because they display some very general characteristics of divination which are usually obscured. Such circular checks may not be universal, but they provide a limiting-case, which I think may be of help in the description of the relationship established, in the participants' minds, between the state of affairs described and its divinatory description.

71

In other words, they constitute cases, in which some properties of divinatory diagnoses are particularly salient.

Situations and their description: the causal link

As we have seen, ancestors in the Sisala and Mundang examples are both the subject matter of divination, which the assertions are supposed to describe, and the entities that make divination possible. I will now try to make this point more general, and examine its consequences as concerns the link, established in the clients' minds, between the state of affairs described and the description itself. My hypothesis is that what the diviner states, with the help of various technical procedures, is considered true insofar as it can be represented as a picture influenced by the very entities described (however indirect the influence). This suggests that such influences are the criterion of true mantic statements in general; the case of meta-divination is special only in that this aspect is clearly displayed at the surface of the ritual.

This is clearer perhaps in the Sisala case. A divination session could be described as a ritual giving a certain picture of the ancestors and their relationship to the client. This picture could be judged on its own merit, as a more or less accurate description of the situation. However, the second divination suggests a very different idea: the justification for performing a checking procedure is that the ancestors can actually 'cheat' and distort a mantic diagnosis; what the second ritual is supposed to establish is whether they allowed the first divination to be accurate. Thus, the combination of two rituals suggests that the diviner's diagnosis is not only a *description* of the ancestors but also a *consequence* of their action (or abstention).

These remarks apply also to the other examples mentioned. In the Mundang case, for instance, the series of ordinary questions, about the client's situation, might be described as just giving a certain description. The ancestors are what the divination is about, and the diagnosis tells in what state the ancestors are as concerns the client and his or her endeavours. The first four questions, however, suggest a different picture. Here the ancestors are entities which cause the divinatory diagnosis. The fact that only they can disrupt it implies, conversely, that they are instrumental in making the diagnosis what it is in the end. This is also implied in the Tallensi case: the ancestors are agencies which both bring about the diagnosis and are described in that diagnosis. It is important to note that establishing this double link, between the situation described and the diagnosis, does not necessarily imply any intention on the ancestors' part. The Mambila example gives a good illustration of that. Here the divinatory pots themselves are 'asked' whether they are truthful; this is conceived as a mechanical operation. If the pot is truthful, then it answers the preliminary questions in the right way, and that's that.

72

My claim here is that the value of mantic statements is evaluated on the basis of an implicit *causal* criterion. Clients and diviners consider the rituals as procedures which make it possible to obtain statements that are directly caused by the situation at hand. A link is established between a certain state of affairs (e.g., the ancestors' attitude to the client, or the fact that so and so is a sorcerer) and the statement which describes this situation. The implicit premise is that the state of affairs itself makes it impossible for the statement to be otherwise; the hidden or unobservable situation causes the statement to be the way it is. Let us not forget that the link is established, in the client's mind, between an undefined and unobservable state of affairs, on the one hand, and a given assertion which describes it, on the other. My claim is that the clients trust the divinatory description because they assume that it is caused by that undefined state of affairs.

To return to the French case studied by Favret and Contreras, if the queen of spades comes up rather than the knave of hearts, this event is linked to the fact that someone is busy trying to bewitch the client; and the link postulated is, I think, of a causal nature. What is strongly implied in the divinatory situation is that, given the human situation at hand, the cards could not have been drawn otherwise. Again, the participants imply that the situation, whatever it is, has provoked the specific patterns displayed by the cards.

The advantage of this interpretation is that it brings together the positive aspects of both anthropological models of divination. In my discussion of the 'intentional' paradigm, I pointed out that the exclusion of the actual speaker's intentions is a crucial feature of divinatory communication. Now the problem is that the usual anthropological inference, that this exclusion is supposed to make room for another, hidden speaker's intentions, is plainly false. We can see now why diviners are so explicit about the fact that their intentions are immaterial. If my interpretation is correct, the divinatory technique is interpreted as a technique which allows situations to speak for themselves, as it were. In this context, excluding the speaker's intentions can be interpreted by the diviners and clients as a way of removing any obstacles on that path. This may also explain why, in many cases, the guarantees of truth of divinatory rituals are mainly negative. What matters is that the ancestors or the spirits or witchcraft will not disrupt the divinatory process. This can be easily understood in the causal framework presented here. Since the main idea is to let a situation cause an utterance about it, any intervention, besides that of the technique itself, can only be conceived of as an interference.

Moreover, this interpretation allows us to understand the inescapable limitation of the semiotic paradigm. It is certainly possible to describe omens or portents as 'signs' of certain situations, insofar as they are interpreted as standing for them in certain circumstances. It should be added, however, that these signs must not be construed as signs in the ordinary sense, i.e., as symbols, but rather as indices, to use Peirce's famous distinction. Their relationship to what they stand for is one of effect to cause.

This interpretation applies to both inspired and mechanical divination. In cases of inspired divination, where, for example, a priestess is supposed to give a message from the god, there is a direct causal link between the state of the god, notably his alleged mental states, and the utterance about them. In mechanical divination, as we have seen, the situation itself is part of the causal process which brings about the utterance concerning it. Both types of divination imply the idea of a causal link between the state of affairs people want to know about and a description of that state of affairs. Moreover, this interpretation allows us to ignore another blurred anthropological distinction, between divination as a technical operation and the interpretation of 'natural' omens. Purely 'natural' omens, even if they are more of an ideal type than a proper category, seem to provide a simple example of the causal connections described above. In the interpretation of omens, most anthropologists accept a version of what I have called the semiotic model of divination. The main idea is that omens are interpreted as *signs* of things to come, and that people who interpret omens are engaged in an operation of decoding. The idea of 'signs', however, is intrinsically ambiguous and does not make the link between signified and signifier precise enough for analytical purposes. Again, what is sometimes described in anthropological theories as a semiotic link, is certainly conceived of by the participants in causal terms. In the case of omens, the assumed causal relation links an original state of affairs and two effects, only one of which is observable; omens are indirect evidence. The flight of the birds can allow one to predict the demise of the empire because the state of affairs (whatever it is) that has made the birds fly this specific way is the one that will make the empire fall.[8] The idea of linking two effects to a single, undefined cause is in fact a very common procedure. When entering a room filled with smoke and with a peculiar smell, people would normally ascribe both to a single cause, even if they cannot identify what is the origin of both phenomena.

To recapitulate, I have tried to show that a precise description of the link between situation and diagnosis may both solve the question of the veracity of divination and show the limitations of common anthropological interpretations. In my view, when a divinatory diagnosis is asked about an unobservable situation, what is assumed is that, in certain circumstances, *it is possible to make statements the content of which is governed by the very situations they describe.* This assumption, I would claim, is always implicit in the participants' representation of the specific discourse situation of divinatory rituals. Besides this general assumption, subjects can have extremely varied descriptions of the specific divinatory procedures available in their cultural environment. In some traditional contexts there is a 'local theory' (in fact some vague representations) about how divination works:

ancestors 'push' the diviner's wand, spirits force the beheaded chicken to run away, and so on. These ideas constitute attempts to describe the causal chain which is implied by the very operation of divination. People may thus conceive a particular ritual as the reception of 'messages' from gods, spirits or ancestors; they may also construe the divinatory technique as the decipherment of 'signs' and 'signatures'. In societies where personified gods are attributed all human characteristics, and supposed to be actively concerned with human affairs, it is no surprise that divination should be interpreted as receiving messages from these anthropomorphic entities. On the other hand, when a group, like in the French Bocage example, has virtually eliminated the transcendent personnel, the causal principle is not expressed in any other idiom than that of pure necessity: given a certain hidden situation, the divinatory diagnosis just could not be otherwise. These reasonings are sometimes made explicit, and accepted by most participants; they may also be mere individual rationalizations.

Such reasonings constitute the specific criteria of truth applied to divinatory situations. If the situations are described in those terms, then the statements generated are likely to be conceived of as more reliable than ordinary discourse, which depends on the speakers' knowledge and intentions, among other factors. In spite of their obvious differences, these specific descriptions always presuppose the causal nature of the link between a situation and its divinatory description. In other words, people assume that the situation, whatever it is, makes the divinatory statement be the way it is. This is the main point for a general anthropological account of divination.

Implicit causal concepts

The hypothesis presented here may seem complicated and 'expensive', in that it attributes to the actors concerned a set of subtle hypotheses, about situations, statements and their connections. This, however, is not the case. As we saw in chapter 3, people do not need explicit general hypotheses about truth and reality, in order to have specific criteria of truth. In much the same way, people who take divinatory diagnoses as the consequence of the situations they describe do not need theoretical elaborations. I am only claiming that their representation of the divinatory utterance is, implicitly, a causal one, and in most circumstances it is bound to remain implicit or unconscious. This point is crucial to the explanation of divination as a criterion of truth, and will be extended to other forms of traditional discourse in the following chapters. It is therefore pertinent to determine exactly what cognitive processes are implied here.

The anthropological study of causal thinking is somehow paradoxical. On the one hand, causal inferences are obviously central in the description of cultures. Describing a specific cultural environment implies focusing, to a large extent, on causal inferences that seem plausible in that environment and would not be admitted elsewhere. It seems self-evident to the Fang that many cases of misfortune can be attributed to specific intentions on the part of the deceased persons (*bekong*), a claim which would appear highly implausible to French Bocage diviners and their clients. A crucial task of any ethnographic description is therefore to explain how subjects are led to consider certain specific causal inferences as plausible or natural. This question, however, is not the subject of much anthropological reflection or speculation. As Needham points out (1976: 80), 'although the notion of cause has been central, since the nineteenth century, to anthropological disquisitions on primitive thought, the modes of causality as conceived in alien traditions have yet to be determined'. Although I cannot engage here in a detailed survey of anthropological ideas on the topic,[9] it may be relevant to examine some of the intellectual factors that led to this strange state of affairs.

Most anthropological ideas on causal thinking were elaborated in the context of the study of 'primitive' or 'magical' thinking; they were therefore focused exclusively on 'strange' causal inferences, e.g., the idea that reciting a certain spell can cure a disease or make the rain fall. In such contexts people make causal connections which seem entirely different from those they find plausible in everyday life. It seems therefore plausible that there must be formal differences between these domains. The very concept of *cause*, and the principles following which an event A can be selected as the cause of event B, must be different. The only difficulty with this approach is that it implies:

(i) that there is a strong, constraining concept of 'cause' used in everyday life, with abstract principles which specify under what conditions events can be considered as causally related;

(ii) that we *know* what these principles are.

The history of philosophical speculation on causality is a strident refutation of claim (ii); however refined the conceptions of causality, they never encompass the variety of causal connections made in everyday life. As for claim (i), cognitive studies tend to show that judgements of causal connections are not made on the basis of abstract rules, about, e.g., the contiguity of events or the fact that the connection considered can be subsumed under a general covering law. Rather, connections are hypothesised on the basis of their resemblance to core cases of simple, observable causal processes, and of their compatibility with general empirical assumptions. To take a very simple example, judging that the impact of the stone thrown at the window caused it to break implies resorting to empirical generalities, e.g., about the relative breakability of glass and stone, besides abstract considerations of spatial contiguity and chronological succession. On their own, such abstract principles would generate indefinitely many causal connections which are never represented by subjects.[10] All this tends to show that anthropological discussions are wrong in assuming that 'strange' causal inferences are rooted in a specific 'mode of thought', somehow divergent from everyday causal thinking. It is difficult to say precisely what such inferences diverge from. Everyday notions of causality seem flexible enough to admit many 'strange' claims, provided there are enough background representations to make the resulting explanations plausible.

Another defect of anthropological ideas on causality is that they focus on *explicit* causal attributions, on situations for instance in which people state that the rains came because the rainmaker performed the appropriate ritual. However, a study of the cognitive processes involved must take into account the fact that many everyday notions are *implicitly* causal. Understanding such basic notions as 'pushing', 'pulling' or 'killing' implies representing intrinsically causal relations. This point, as we will see presently, is directly relevant to my argument on divination and other traditional forms of discourse.

To sum up, anthropological discussions of causality often neglect everyday causal attributions and hypothesise specific cognitive mechanisms, specialised in 'magical' and other such 'symbolic' reasonings. But the common processes may well be powerful and flexible enough to accommodate most of the 'strange' connections people seem to find plausible. I will take this possibility as a starting point in the discussion of traditional criteria of truth. Although what is said here is not meant as a thorough discussion of 'magic', which is outside the scope of our problem, I hope it will convey the message that anthropological theories on such phenomena should be based on clear and plausible cognitive hypotheses rather than as *ad hoc* constructions.

To return to our specific problem, I have suggested here that people involved in the interpretation of a divinatory statement evaluate it by positing a causal link between the (undefined) situation at hand and the diagnosis that describes it. The process of evaluating certain descriptions or representations, on the basis of implicit *causal* criteria, rather than *descriptive* ones, is in fact present in very simple everyday activities. A good illustration, which is often used in philosophical discussions, is the way we commonly evaluate photographs.[11] It may seem that a photograph of, e.g., Kensington Palace counts as a photograph of that building because of its resemblance to the original: the picture has the same parts, the same proportions and the same ornaments as a given perspective of the real building. This would mean that the picture is judged solely on its descriptive link to the object represented, namely Kensington Palace. This, however, is not the case. Imagine the picture is taken with the wrong exposure, on the wrong type of film, with the wrong lens, etc., so that it is difficult to see anything on the resulting image, let alone to see what the picture is a picture of. Such a photograph would still be a photograph of Kensington Palace, although a bad one. On the other hand, a picture of a model of Kensington Palace, whatever its resemblance to the real building, would never count as a photograph of Kensington Palace. 'Being a photograph of' is therefore an intrinsically *causal* notion, which applies only if the light reflected by the original object has reached the film and caused chemical changes in it. This assumption is implicit in the ordinary understanding of the notion, even if people do not necessarily know how light reaches the film or effects those chemical changes.

In the interpretation of divination offered here, the participants' representation of divination is, in the same way, implicitly causal. Understanding the difference between ordinary and divinatory discourse, for the subjects concerned, implies representing the latter as caused by the situations represented. As we can see in the case of photographs, subjects who assume a causal connection between an object or situation and its representation, do not necessarily have an elaborate 'theory' of the connection. They assume that it exists, but do not necessarily represent what it consists of.

The hypothesis of causal criteria has many implications for the study of traditional truths. Let me mention one immediate consequence, the relevance of which I will examine in the next chapter. In this account of divinatory truths, truth-terms are applied, not to sentences or propositions, but to singular *utterances*. I am referring here to the distinction between a sentence, i.e., an abstract reality generated by some grammar, and an utterance, a physical realisation of the sentence.[12] It is generally agreed that truth predicates apply to sentences or rather to the propositions they express in a given language, so that the idea of judging an utterance 'true' without applying criteria of truth to the sentence expressed may seem strange. This, however, is a consequence of the special nature of causal criteria. When using causal criteria, people necessarily focus their reasonings on the utterance as an event. Worryingly, this seems to suggest that the *content* of the utterances is not always the most important factor in the processes whereby they are judged 'true'. If this is the case, then it should be possible to judge 'true' an utterance whose content is virtually eliminated. This possibility is indeed exploited in certain forms of traditional discourse, to which we shall now turn.

5
Customised speech (II): truth without meaning

Although traditions are commonly supposed to imply beliefs, conceptions and world views, traditional contexts are difficult to describe in these terms. More often than not, the aspects of discourse which are linked to the expression of underlying ideas and beliefs about the world are secondary or irrelevant, while the salient aspects are precisely not expressive in that sense. In chapter 2, I examined a crucial feature of the categories used in traditional interaction, namely that they are anchored to memories of singular situations rather than associated with mental definitions. As a consequence, expert utterances about these notions rely on the undefined resemblance between situations, rather than general propositions about the world. This is but an aspect of a general property of traditional discourse, which is *ritualised* in a variety of ways. Now, as Rappaport points out, an 'obvious aspect' of ritual and ritualised interaction is that they are non−discursive and non-explanatory (1974 *passim*).

I will now turn to a striking example of 'non-expressivity' in traditions, namely the use of formalised or ritualised languages. In many traditional contexts truths are supposedly contained in utterances which the listeners, sometimes even the speakers, can barely understand. The discourse itself thus constitutes an obstacle to the 'expression' of underlying 'ideas'. Such phenomena cannot be just explained away as exceptions; in many societies, they are the hallmark of traditional truth. A theory of traditional discourse should therefore account for this limiting case, where truth seems to be compatible with virtually meaningless utterances.

Ritual speech

Ritual speech may be construed as an intermediary form between two other manipulations of language, viz. the construction of special languages and the use of spells. Special languages range from argots and professional jargons to the complex secret idioms used in some initiations and secret societies. They are used in various ways, to serve as identity markers or to make secret communication possible. They are generally formed on the basis of a natural language, which is made incomprehensible to the outsiders by various formal processes, like morphological transformations, the systematic use of a repertoire of metaphors, a vocabulary either invented or taken from a foreign tongue, often in combination.[1] Spells and other gnomic forms, on the other hand, are an extreme form of the formulaic use of language. By virtue of being repeated in a certain form or in certain contexts, some more or less obscure formulae are supposed to have other properties, notably other effects, than ordinary speech. In a sense, spells and secret languages are symmetrical distortions of natural language. The point in using a special language is to create or emphasise differences in the code used, whatever the message. Spells on the contrary stress the difference between different possible uses of the same language.

Ritual speech functions in both directions. On the one hand, it makes use of linguistic forms which are markedly distinct from ordinary speech; also, it is only used in specific contexts, where utterances are supposed to be more salient than in ordinary conversation. As we will see in the examples and hypotheses presented below, ritual speech is usually described as more efficient; its use in ritual contexts is often meant to have a material effect on some situation. Most studies of ritual speech focus on this aspect. Here, however, I will deal with another puzzling aspect, with the relationship established between ritual speech and truth. In most cases, what is said in the ritual idiom, using the appropriate formulae, is supposed to convey some truth which cannot be expressed in ordinary discourse. The problem then is to understand the combination of ritualisation and veracity.

A good illustration of this combination is Cuna formalised speech, as described by Sherzer (1985). Among the Cuna of Panama, all knowledge beyond common sense is embodied in various forms of ritualised discourse; knowing more than other people means knowing certain songs and formulae, and being able to master certain formalised styles. The Cuna emphasis on ritual discourse is extreme; there is very little ritual activity besides these formalised verbal genres. Cuna tradition as a whole is thus constituted by three types of discourse and contexts, associated with the chiefs' oratory, the healing rites and the girls' puberty rites respectively (Sherzer 1985: 22ff.). There are ritual specialists and a specific form of discourse associated with each of these contexts; the special vocabulary used, as well as specific morphological and syntactic rules and the introduction of parallelism, make ritual discourse virtually unintelligible for non-specialists; there are thus three different special languages, which specialists learn by memorising songs and incantations.

The chiefs' discourse is especially interesting here, as it is supposed both to convey important truths about the past and to set people good examples to follow in everyday life. Chiefs only make this type of speech in the formalised context of the common house (*namakke*) meetings; every other night the whole population of the village gathers there and listens to these speeches, usually structured as a dialogue between two chiefs. The subject matter is mainly mythological and cosmological, although it incorporates descriptions of recent events or of the chiefs' experiences and various other stories. The content of such dialogues is by no means stereotyped, and there is a good deal of improvisation; the style, however, is always that of formal oratory. The language used by the chiefs is barely intelligible to the listeners. After the chiefs' dialogue, which usually lasts for about two hours, two specialised interpreters give a shortened translation and some comments on the meaning of the narratives (Sherzer 1985: 72ff.).

In this context, much emphasis is laid on the truths contained in the chiefs' discourse. It must be stressed that this aspect is clearly conceived of as distinct from the strictly political role played by the chiefs. In certain villages the functions are fulfilled by different chiefs; some of them, more knowledgeable in mythological matters, make these ritualised speeches, while others are concerned with the management of day-to-day activities (Sherzer 1985: 57). Ritualised discourse is thus considered mainly as a source of true statements about the past and present states of village life. This aspect is of course difficult to combine with the fact that ritualised utterances are made in a language which most listeners cannot understand at all. They are provided with a translation, but the original is considered to be true, not the translation. Relevant aspects can be explained by the translators, but it is necessary to resort to the formalised register beforehand.[2]

This has an important consequence, which in fact applies to most cases of ritualised speech: the utterances are supposed to convey a truth not in spite of, but *because of* their formalisation. This of course goes against the common idea, that such forms of discourse consist in the expression of world-views or other cultural 'conceptions'. If we analyse ritual discourse in this way, we are led to focus on aspects which are either nonexistent or irrelevant, while the aspects considered crucial by the actors, notably the formalisation, are just ignored. In a common conception of traditions, such institutions are therefore incomprehensible.[3] We must therefore examine whether a different view would make it possible to account for this puzzling aspect of traditional discourse.

The obvious problem with ritual speech is that it seems paradoxical. The more formalised the utterances, the more they are conceived of as containing some truth. At the same time however, more formalised utterances are necessarily more difficult to understand, and this is often pushed to an extreme point, where the utterances are totally incomprehensible. How does one get truth with less meaning or no meaning at all? If people's criteria of truth are supposed to be descriptive, to be about the states of affairs described by the sentences, there is no way to account for this paradox; one must either ignore the facts or distort them. Here I will try to show that an alternative hypothesis on criteria of truth could provide a solution to the paradox and account for the connection between truth and obscure ritualised forms.

Formalisation and force: Bloch's hypothesis

The combination of formalisation and cognitive salience is the subject matter of an important argument put forward by M. Bloch (1974), which I shall examine in some detail in this and the following section. Bloch's argument is founded on an ethnographic analysis of two types of Merina ritual discourse, associated with political oratory and circumcision rites respectively. The argument suggests that these types of discourse, although clearly different in their aim and context, have many similarities; and that the mechanism of persuasion of religious discourse uses some of the 'coercive' devices of traditional authority. I shall first present a brief summary of Bloch's ideas on ritual languages, and then comment on some consequences of these hypotheses.

Bloch's strong hypothesis is that the type of cognitive effect which is achieved by ritual statements is a consequence of formalisation. There is not just a connection between these aspects, one is a consequence of the other. Formalised speech conveys less information about the world than ordinary speech, but it achieves another type of communicative effect, which depends on other aspects of the utterances, namely their 'illocutionary properties'. Formalisation can be seen as a modification of normal speech which reduces its information-conveying potential and by the same token enhances its illocutionary potential; the effects of ritual speech on the audience are proportional to the reduction of the information transmitted. The idea of course is directly opposed to what most theories of tradition would predict, on the assumption that traditional discourse expresses some underlying ideas about the world, so that statements which express very little should not be considered by the actors as especially important and traditional. Contrary to this, Bloch argues that both aspects, formalisation and salience, are not only found together but are strongly connected. In his terms, 'with increasing formalisation, propositional force decreases and illocutionary force increases' (Bloch 1974: 67).

This idea of an inversed proportion is founded on a specific description of the formalisation of ritual languages. The main idea is that ritual formalisation or stylisation results in constraining the creative power of language; not all sentences meet the prosodic or morphological requirements of the ritual style. As a consequence, ritual languages are impoverished languages. In Bloch's conception, the propositional force of a sentence is described in terms very close to the idiom of information theory. Any given sentence is a consequence of some paradigmatic choices among sets of possible sentences; the quantity of information conveyed by a sentence is inversely proportional to the probability of the choice made.[4] The more probable (and consequently predictable) the sentence, the less informative. Stylisation is a reduction in the number of possible choices, so that the utterances are far more predictable than in ordinary speech; the stylistic constraints are such that, from one sentence, the listeners can predict what follows; 'if this mode of communication is adopted there is hardly any *choice* of what can be said' (Bloch 1974: 62). The loss of choice, and the consequent increase of predictability, are an essential feature of any stylisation, and formalised ritual speech is an extreme example of this process.

In some cases the formalisation is such that there is no choice at all; given a certain point of departure, a speech-act A, and a certain compulsory style, speakers cannot but make the totally predictable speech act B. To use Bloch's image, engaging in such a discourse is like being in a tunnel; having no possibility to turn either left or right, the only thing one can do is to follow (Bloch 1974: 76). This allows Bloch to describe ritual language as intrinsically coercive. The actors are 'caught' in a discursive pattern which makes it impossible to disagree or contradict, since the series of utterances is predetermined from the outset. The choice for the actor, then, is between accepting the conventions of discourse, thereby accepting the imposed utterances, and not speaking at all. As Bloch himself points out, this of course is a limiting-case; formalisation is usually not complete; still, the extent to which it restricts the possibilities of a speech act B is 'the limit within which contradiction is possible' (Bloch 1974: 64). Ritual language can thus serve an ideological purpose, in that it is a 'hidden' yet powerful mechanism which reduces drastically the possibility of dissent.[5]

Beyond the detailed analysis of Merina political discourse, Bloch's interpretation relies on some general assumptions that deserve a detailed discussion. Against most anthropological ideas on ritual discourse, it contends that veracity, in such contexts, is a direct consequence of formalisation. The hypothesis seems far more plausible than common anthropological ideas on discourse in ritual. The general premises, however, are not entirely satisfactory. In order to give a general and plausible account of ritual speech, it is therefore necessary to examine the precise claims made about the cognitive effects of utterances.

First, let me mention some empirical problems concerning the application of the hypotheses. They concern a very specific type of situation, in which various participants take part in what is presented as a debate but, due to the formalisation of discourse, does not in fact leave room for contradiction. The model should be qualified if it is meant to apply to cases where the distribution of roles is entirely different, and where the tie-on of persuasion with coercion is not so obvious. In the Cuna case, for example, the chiefs' ritualised discourse is supposed to convey some truth and it is highly formalised. But the listeners, who take these utterances as true, are not meant to engage themselves in ritualised replies. In other words, there are cases (perhaps more representative of ritual speech than Merina political oratory) where the juxtaposition of ritual formalisation and cognitive effects does not rely on the fact that people are forced to 'participate' in the discourse, quite the contrary. Shall we count out these phenomena as entirely different from Bloch's example? This would be odd, given the obvious and significant similarities. If we find in many areas of traditional discourse a combination of formalisation and psychological salience or other such effects, this surely deserves a general explanation. But then we must modify some features of Bloch's ingenious model.

The hypothesis of an inversed proportion is problematical, in that it suggests that strong illocutionary effects are an automatic consequence of the reduction of propositional choice. This is obviously false, and many counter-examples can be found. In a conversation with someone who has a limited command of the language, the choice of words is obviously reduced to the most common or basic expressions; utterances made in such conversations are not especially 'strong' at the illocutionary level, quite the contrary. Indirect speech acts, irony and other such effects are ruled out. Therefore the relationship between these two aspects is more complex. Ritual formalisation, in Bloch's sense, must be construed as weak propositional choice combined with some awareness of other, non-reduced, types of discourse. Speakers must be aware of what they could have said in a non-formalised style and cannot say in ritual language.

Even granted this common sense addition, the idea of a systematic relation seems problematical. It implies that a genre of ritual speech which is more formalised is bound to have more effects than other types. But the evidence does not seem to support this. Very formalised utterances are sometimes found with minimal effects; conversely, a highly inventive discourse can result in strong effects. In the Fang syncretic *bwiti* religion, the most persuasive sermons turn out to be based on the invention of ingenious metaphors rather than on formalised talk (Fernandez 1986: 28–70, 172–86) and there are of course many such examples. This implies that Bloch's hypothesis is not false, but incomplete. The idea that formalisation entails truth is insufficient, given the counter-examples, but it will give us the starting point of a plausible solution.

In order to go further, it may be of help to remember that the analysis of divinatory speech posed a similar problem. Divinatory statements are said to be true *because* they are produced by the divinatory operations. Most anthropological models just ignore this and try to describe the institution as though statements were produced *in spite of* the procedures.[6] On the other hand, the idea that clients find true whatever is said by diviners just begs the question. What we must do is describe the additional assumptions which, if admitted, make it possible to consider divinatory operations as truth-making. In other words, divination does not produce truth, unless one has some implicit hypotheses about how it works. This, as we will see, is also what happens in the case of ritual language. Veracity is taken by the listeners as necessarily linked to formalisation, and Bloch's model is an attempt to take this fact into account. But veracity would not be seen as a consequence of formalisation if people did not have specific hypotheses about the way the utterances are produced. A satisfactory account of formal language must describe these hypotheses.

Illocutionary force: a problem of description

Bloch's account is founded on a distinction between propositional and illocutionary forces, two notions widely used in pragmatics. However, each of these terms is taken here in a special sense, and I shall argue that some problems in this explanation of ritual language stem from this particular conception of the interpretation of utterances.[7] The force of ritual utterances cannot be explained in propositional terms; formalisation reduces the 'propositional potential' of sentences to a minimum. In Bloch's model, the effects on the audience, such as persuasion or coercion, must be attributed to the illocutionary interpretation of the utterances. In this conception, illocutionary force is conceived as some kind of energy, something which an utterance can have more or less of, i.e., something which resembles 'forces' in the ordinary, physical sense. Now this is a far cry from most pragmatic accounts of illocution.[8] In pragmatic theory in general, illocution is not seen at all as a force in that sense; this point deserves some attention, as it is crucial in the question of ritual speech. A fundamental idea of speech-act theory is the distinction between locutionary and illocutionary aspects of an utterance. Sentences can be classified as declarative, interrogative, imperative, etc.; these are locutionary aspects. Now these aspects do not determine the illocutionary aspects, e.g., interpreting the utterance as a request, a statement, etc. Suppose one enters a very hot room, points at the window and tells the people sitting there: 'A bit stuffy in here, isn't it?' The sentence itself is a combination of a declarative and an interrogative sentence; these are its locutionary aspects. Now, at the illocutionary level, the utterance obviously can be interpreted neither as a statement, as the other people are supposed to know that it is hot, nor as a genuine question. It is intended as an indirect request, something which could be also expressed by, e.g., 'would you mind opening a window?' and it is interpreted as such. The important point here is that the illocutionary aspects of an utterance are qualities like, e.g., being a request, an order, a wish, a statement. These are qualities an utterance has or has not, they are not quantities it could have more or less of. An utterance cannot be more of a request than another one; it is or it is not a request. The very term 'illocutionary *force*' is misleading, in that it suggests some variable quantity, whereas one is dealing with aspects which would be more properly described as modalities.

Bloch's idea of an inversed proportion of propositional and illocutionary 'forces' means that both can vary in quantity. This may apply to propositional potential, insofar as it is described in information-theoretic terms, but certainly not to illocutionary aspects. It may be of help here to resort to another distinction made by Austin, between illocutionary and 'perlocutionary' aspects (1962: 100–7). In the example, mentioned above, making an indirect request is the illocutionary act; now the effects this act has on the people in the room are yet another matter. They might react, e.g., by opening a window, by protesting that it is not hot at all, or by making another indirect speech-act, saying for instance: 'I happen to have a very bad cold.' All such effects pertain to the perlocutionary aspects of the utterance. In the problem of ritual speech we obviously need some distinction of this sort. The utterances made have certain illocutionary aspects; they constitute orders, advice, statements and so on. What is of more interest to the anthropologist, however, is the effect of the utterances on the listeners. Ritual utterances are extremely salient, they are described as conveying some truth, they can be used to convince people. In his account, Bloch considers all such aspects (together with 'illocution' in the usual, narrow sense) as part of the 'illocutionary force' of an utterance.[9] In order to account for the persuasion effects of some utterances, Bloch needs to describe parallelism as a mechanism which precludes the possibility of alternative messages. But there are many cases of parallelism without this characteristic. So the persuasiveness of ritualised speech must depend, not only on the properties of the utterances, but also on the listeners' representations about the utterances and the domain of reality which is talked about.

Utterances as events and instantiations

In both linguistic theory and everyday understanding, utterances can be considered from two quite different points of view. On the one hand, utterances are concrete instantiations of certain abstract objects, namely sentences, illocutionary forces, conversational maxims and so on. An utterance, however, is also a simple singular *event*. Someone saying something at a certain location constitutes an event which is liable to be caused by other events or states of affairs. The Fang witch-doctor's assertion that ant-hills mean witchcraft (made at a specific time before a specific audience) is an instantiation of the sentence 'ant-hills mean witchcraft' which expresses some abstract proposition about a relationship between ant-hills and witchcraft. However, it can also be described as a singular event that is located in both time and space and can be memorised as such, as the person so and so making the statement such and such in such and such singular situation.

This distinction is relevant to the problem of parallelism and other such procedures used in ritual languages. Such transformations of natural language have two consequences. They make it difficult to interpret the utterances as the expression of sentences, because of the lack of expressive power described by Bloch. At the same time, some surface properties of the utterances become highly salient; parallelism displays at the surface of the utterances some syntactic or morphological or phonological structures which are usually unnoticeable. The Kham-Magar shamanistic songs collected and studied by A. de Sales in Nepal (1986) are a good illustration of this phenomenon. They are sung by the shamans in a special language, with a very poor vocabulary (not more than a thousand words, mainly of Nepali origin) and a simplified syntax, and make a constant use of parallelistic constructions. Take for instance the following recurrent formula (Sales 1985; 317):

Purai purkha na pura wastri nga
Whole husband you whole wife I

which is glossed as 'You are my legitimate husband, I am your legitimate wife.' In ordinary Kham-Magar language, this would be rendered by the sentence:

Na purai nga purkha nalizya, na purai na wastri ngalizya
You whole mine husband you-are, I whole yours wife I-am.

In this example, the transformation from ordinary to ritual language concerns both morphology and syntax. There is no verb in the ritual formula, and the juxtaposition of the elements in a single line is supposed to replace the copula. In the same way,

Naza sakina na naza bakina na
You you-can you, you you-speak you

is glossed as 'you are the one who can speak', a proposition whose complexity is far beyond the possibilities of the ritual syntax. As Sales puts it, words in the ritual language seem to be 'handled like objects' (Sales 1985: 317), as independent units that can be juxtaposed or separated for reasons other than syntactical.

These are very common characteristics of ritualised speech. In the space of this chapter it is not possible to present a detailed description of parallelistic and other distortions, or to enter into the description of their cognitive effects. Two points, however, must be noted, because they are directly relevant to the question of truth. First, listeners who do not master the basic vocabulary of such songs recognise them as series of utterances rather than noise only by virtue of the strong prosodic organisation; this poetry is always 'opaque' in the sense that it is impossible to interpret it without focusing on surface properties like, e.g., the recurrence of certain phonological combinations.[10] Second, inasmuch as listeners have some knowledge of the limited vocabulary, they are bound to focus on the iconic aspects of parallelistic constructions. There is a strong, inevitable element of iconicity in ritual speech, if only because the vocabulary and syntax are not rich enough to express all the thoughts conveyed. Thus, Sales points out that the unity of the mythic couple, in the sentence 'Whole husband you whole wife I,' is suggested by the syntactic structure itself, by the juxtaposition of the words (Sales 1985: 318). Some features of the objects described are supposedly reflected in the surface properties of the utterances. Predication is often conveyed by contiguity, opposition by prosodic breaks, and so on. As a result, the listener's interpretation of ritual speech, if the latter is treated as something other than random noise, is necessarily focused on the properties of the utterances as phonic *events*, as material occurrences. At the same time, the obscurity and ambiguity of formalised utterances make it more difficult to interpret them as the realisation of abstract objects, notably of sentences. If we take this into account, it may be possible to complete Bloch's model and put forward a general account of truth in formalised language.

Ritual speech as caused utterances

In chapter 4, I put forward the hypothesis that divinatory operations can be taken as an argument for truth only if the listeners assume that the diagnosis is *caused* by the very situation it describes. In other words, the fact that divination is persuasive is not a direct consequence of its formal properties; it is a consequence of the availability, in the listeners' minds, of a causal description of these formal properties. People do not judge divination truthful simply because it is divination, but because they have an implicit causal assumption, in which the statement is caused by the undefined situation at hand.

Applying this interpretation to the case of ritual speech would imply that the persuasive effects are not attributed to parallelism as such, but to the fact that people interpret formalised utterances as caused by the very states of affairs or entities they describe. Formalisation would be represented by people as an index of the fact that the utterances produced are influenced or triggered by ancestors, witchcraft, spirits, etc. This assumption can be entertained only if the listeners have representations about both the existence of a causal link and the fact that formalisation is its index. They must have (i) some representation of the fact that the ancestors, spirits and other entities described are actually instrumental in bringing about the utterances concerned, and (ii) some representation of the surface properties of the formalised utterances as a consequence of this process.

Bloch's own description of Merina ritual oratory seems to bear out this causal interpretation. The rituals begin with some elders explaining the purpose of the ceremony, in a style which is closely similar to that of ordinary political oratory. A notable change occurs, however, as the ritual proceeds. The speeches delivered after a few hours are very different from political oratory, in content as well as style; they tend to be indistinct and more parallelistic than at the beginning. 'They would be classed [by the observer] as the speeches of persons under possession. The elders appear to be in a trance-like state...' (Bloch 1985: 58). At no stage, in these speeches, are the elders supposed to speak on their own behalf; what they are saying are 'the words of the ancestors'. People apply this description to both the speeches of the beginning, which sound like political oratory, and the subsequent, 'possession-sounding' discourse. At both stages, the words of the ancestors are supposedly realised by the elders' utterances: 'for them possession is an extreme form of saying what would have been said by the elders of the past, or repeating their words' (Bloch, 1985: 59). There is a marked difference, however, between the two stages, as Bloch points out: 'instead of the ancestors speaking *indirectly* through the *memory* of the living elders they speak *directly* through their *person*' (1985, Bloch's emphasis).

This type of change seems to suggest that the elders' utterances gradually become more directly influenced by the ancestors themselves. Instead of repeating what they think were ancient sentences, the speakers are forced to utter what the ancestors make them say. Bloch emphasises the fact that the connection between the ancestors and the elders' speech gradually becomes a direct one. At the beginning of the ritual, the elders are supposed to be quoting what they can remember. As the ritual proceeds, however, they are by-passed, as it were, in a process which links what the ancestors want to say and what the elders actually utter. This is an obvious feature of possession; but I must insist on the fact that in such a form of discourse, what is said is supposed to be directly caused by some entity other than the speakers themselves. If this interpretation is correct, the formalised utterances are systematically interpreted as directly influenced by events or states of affairs which they describe. Most formalised discourse should then be construed as not only a quotation but, more strongly, as the consequence of the reality described. Instead of being a quotation of, e.g., 'the words of the ancestors', formalised utterances in ritual contexts would be interpreted as triggered *by* the ancestors.

It is important at this point not to misunderstand the 'quoted' aspects of ritual discourse. In the Merina case, for instance, it seems that the listeners naturally interpret the formalised utterances as simply spoken by 'someone else', namely the ancestors, through the elders' mouths. Then formalised speech would be just quoted speech, the irruption of some alien speaker in someone's discourse. This is suggested by Sherzer in his interpretation of Cuna ritual speech, which systematically includes reflexive and metacommunicative elements, so that utterances are 'one or more steps (actually one or more mouths) removed from the actual speaker' (1985: 210). I do not want to query the relevance of this interpretation in the specific cases considered; taken as a general principle, however, the hypothesis would be false.

A parallel with divination will make this clearer. As we saw in chapter 4, the clients in certain forms of divination assume that the diagnosis is not produced by the diviner but have no idea who then is 'speaking', and often do not even bother to consider this problem. What is assumed is that, given the (undefined) situation at hand, the diagnosis could not have been otherwise. As I said, the only assumption here is that the diagnosis is caused by the situation. The idea of hidden or divine 'speakers' is not necessary to this causal interpretation; in those cases, however, where the subject-matter of divination is the influence of personified agencies like gods and spirits, is quite natural to interpret the diagnosis as the words of these gods and spirits. The diagnosis is then interpreted as caused by these agencies' intentions. This, however, is just one possible way of describing a causal link between situations and utterances; there are many forms of divination in which a causal link is assumed, without this 'personified' description.

In much the same way, we must be wary of an interpretation which describes the ritual speaker as just a 'spokesman' for spirits or ancestors. There are cases in which formalised speech is supposed to contain some truths, without any hypothesis about the 'hidden speakers' behind the actual ones. The idea that ritual speech is interpreted as the words of mystical entities is therefore too specific, if we want to account for this phenomenon in general. Both personified and non-personified interpretations of ritual speech presuppose the idea of a causal link from an undefined situation to the utterances actually made.

To sum up: what is proposed here is that formalised or parallelistic speech, in these ritual contexts, is taken by the listeners as a form of speech directly influenced by some situation or some entities described. *Pace* Bloch, I would claim that 'reduced propositional potential' on its own, is not sufficient for the utterances to be held true. Semantic vacuity and parallelism are indices of truth only if the listeners have some assumptions about the reasons why discourse is thus distorted. Now parallelism and other types of formalisation focus the listeners' attention on the properties of utterances as events, and therefore make it possible to entertain hypotheses about the utterances as events caused. This, of course, is only one of the effects of parallelism, but it is necessary to take it into account if we want to understand why and how such discourse can be held truthful in spite of its reduced 'propositional potential'.

Truths as a rare commodity

Divination techniques and the ritualisation of speech obviously pose different problems; in both cases, however, traditional truths are created by 'customising' speech. The production of ordinary discourse involves different mechanisms, and the customisation consists in substituting artificial mechanisms for the natural processes at some point in the production of utterances. In divination, this applies to the assumption, following which the content of a statement is usually determined by what a person wishes to express; in such contexts, the speaker's intention is replaced with a technical operation whose result is unpredictable. In the case of ritual speech, this applies to another usual assumption, namely that statements can be understood as describing a certain state of affairs; this principle is demoted and the utterances are consequently represented as patterns of surface features. There are no doubt many other ways of customising discourse; these examples are only two illustrations of the possibilities and results of this process.

The idea of truth criteria being applied to utterances as events caused, rather than sentences expressed, makes it possible to understand an important feature of the traditional style, namely its 'literalism'. In chapter 1, I used the term in an intuitive way, to designate the fact that people want statements made in traditional contexts to be repeated accurately. This emphasis on accuracy implies that a paraphrase of an utterance cannot have quite the same value as a *verbatim* repetition, though both have the same content. What I called 'expert utterances', in Fang discourse, are generally cited in their exact phrasing. People feel that any change in the surface features of the utterance would affect its value. Indeed, the very idea of a paraphrase, of a change that does not affect the truth conditions of the sentence, seems alien to the traditional style. A classical interpretation of these aspects of traditional style is founded on the idea of traditionalism; this may be described as a preference for time-tested conceptions or as an instinctive compulsion of repetition. In chapter 1, I mentioned some of the problems created by this type of psychological explanation, in which people are said to stick to old formulations because they want certain ideas or conceptions to remain unchanged. Applied to the specific question of literalism, such a conception would imply that people prefer *verbatim* repetition because it is a safe way of preserving the ideas or conceptions expressed. But in the limiting case of ritual speech, people are 'literalist' about utterances which have very little 'propositional content', to use Bloch's terms. These are utterances about which it is certainly impossible to represent what the 'content' to be conserved is, since there is virtually none. So literalism cannot be construed as the desire to conserve 'conceptions' and 'meanings'. In the model presented here, there is no need to suppose that people represent some 'conception' which they wish to preserve. Literalism can be understood as a consequence of the choice of causal criteria of truth in certain contexts. Utterances are then considered true insofar as the event of the utterance meets certain requirements, notably if it is possible to represent a causal link between the situation described and the utterance. If such criteria are taken into account, the only reliable utterances are those for which a relevant causal description is available.

An important consequence is that, to use a convenient metaphor, truth is a rare commodity. The number of situations in which it is necessary to find a true description or explanation of a state of affairs greatly outnumbers the number of contexts in which guaranteed truths are produced. There are only a limited number of divination operations or ritual speech sessions, and most of the truths produced only concern very specific questions. So the problem is to extend the applicability of ritually guaranteed statements to other situations. Ideally, this could be done in two different ways, either by inferring new truths on the basis of the ritually guaranteed ones, or by seeking some analogies, between the object of the ritual truths and the new situations at hand. The problem with the first strategy is that it does not offer any guarantee about the truth of what is so deduced. As I pointed out, causal criteria can only apply to *singular* utterances. Once inferences and deductions are made, there is no guarantee that they will be as true as the original statement, because there is no causal link between them and the situation described. The second strategy, seeking resemblance between situations, while quoting the same singular truths, is the very principle of literalism. Let me return again to the example of Fang ant-hills and witchcraft mentioned in chapter 2. The statement was made in such circumstances that it was supposed to be true. Now there are many situations where certainties about witchcraft are in high demand. In such situations, people do not try to extrapolate some general principles from the specific utterance about ant-hills; what they do is quote this original statement, although the situation at hand is quite different. The implicit idea is that there *must* be some resemblance between the two situations, although it is not precisely described.

As I mentioned above, an utterance can be apprehended and described in two different ways, as an instantiation of some abstract object (a sentence) or as a singular speech-event. Both aspects are represented in the listeners' interpretation; an utterance is construed as realising a certain sentence, and it is also an event which has causes, effects and circumstances. As a consequence, literalism is manifest in two typical ways. *Quoting* is the most obvious one; people tend to favor the repetition of an utterance rather than adapting the original to the new circumstances. Quoting an utterance is making another utterance which shares the instantiation properties of the first one; it is a realisation of the same sentence, and consequently people can imagine that it has the same truth-value as the original one. I would argue, however, that due to the existence of criteria focused on events, the quotation of an utterance cannot be considered as obviously true as the utterance itself. This is why another common property of traditional contexts is the *reiteration* of the circumstances which guarantee the truth of the statements. Reiteration focuses on the event properties of the utterance; if a truth has been produced by resorting to a certain technical operation or to a certain type of specialist, then an obvious way to create new truths is to resort to the same type of operations and specialists. In this way, one reproduces the properties of the utterances which make it possible to imagine a causal link between the states of affairs described and the speech-events.

Literalism is, then, more complex than is usually assumed in anthropological descriptions. It does not involve any specially 'conservative' tendency, but is a consequence of the type of criteria used to judge that statements are true. It is also more complex in the sense that two different phenomena are concerned, the prevalence of reported speech and the tendency to reiterate certain circumstances for the expression of truths. These two aspects are not usually described together, although they seem to be two consequences of the same cognitive processes involved in the interpretation of traditional statements.[11]

6

Customised persons: initiation, competence and position

A salient aspect of traditional situations is that the access to truth, more precisely the capacity to make true statements, is reserved for persons placed in certain social positions. If one considers traditional statements as the expression of transmitted 'theories' or 'world-views', there are two ways of explaining why truth-bearing discourse is thus reserved for certain actors. The first solution is to have an 'authoritarian' idea of the groups concerned, i.e., to claim that in such groups whatever is said by the 'powerful' is held true. The second possible solution is that the actors concerned have a special competence, notably a greater knowledge of traditional 'theories' than ordinary speakers. At the end of chapter 3, I mentioned the problems created by the 'authoritarian' interpretation. The main difficulty is that the claim just begs the question of the intellectual processes whereby a person is endowed with traditional 'authority'. If position is a simple criterion of truth, why and how is it considered a criterion? If, for example, shamans are the only ones who can say the truth about the spirits, what are the listeners' representations about this capacity? Apparently, the only reasonable answer to this question is some notion of 'competence'; the privileged speakers have more knowledge than the others. This is the most natural hypothesis; in fact, if the veracity of utterances is evaluated on the basis of their content, it is the only reasonable hypothesis. As we saw in the previous chapters, however, the criteria used in the evaluation of traditional statements are not that simple. They are based on representations which, to some extent, 'by-pass' considerations of content. Indeed, there are limiting cases where content is virtually absent, as we saw in the examination of ritual languages.

Clearly, the idea of 'competence' is more problematic than it first seemed. This is why I will now turn to institutions which are supposed to give some people the capacity of stating the truth, yet are not amenable to a description in terms of 'competence'. This in turn will help us make some hypotheses about the way social positions are represented in traditional interaction. Traditional truths often require a 'customisation' of speech; they also require the special preparation of persons. Here I will consider the most salient example of such preparations, namely the rituals which supposedly

94

create 'new' persons and consequently make them capable of truthful discourse.

The cognitive paradox of initiation and competence

Initiation rites are not easily defined, but their 'family resemblance' is based on a combination of (i) a change of status, supposedly effected by the ritual itself and often expressed in terms of knowledge or access to some information, and (ii) some formal characteristics such as the seclusion of candidates, the secrecy surrounding initiation proceedings, the painful or humiliating ordeals, the use of specialised languages or codes or other means of representations, etc.[1] One of the main anthropological problems is that of the status of initiation *knowledge*. In many societies initiations are said to confer some kind of knowledge, either practical (hunting, fishing, etc.) or mystical (some secrets about ghosts or ancestors or masks). In either case it is difficult to take such presentations of initiation at face value. Most activities 'learned' were in fact largely known, or even practised, by the candidates before their admission. And whatever mystical knowledge is transmitted seems to focus on secrets either meaningless or empty. For instance, neophytes are told that the masks, previously described as mysterious instantiations of ancestors or spirits, are just a gross deception; they are actually worn by fathers, uncles and other male adults.[2] In some cases the communication of secrets can be delayed indefinitely. In the Baktaman initiations described by F. Barth (1975), candidates proceed through a system of grades; what they learn at each step is that the essential secrets, the ultimate explanations, will be given next time. In many initiations candidates have to learn a special language or system of signs, supposed to embody a new, deeper understanding of the world; most of these new semiotic systems boil down to simple rhetorical modifications of the native tongue and the common representations, so that what is learned is either trivial or empty (Boyer 1980: *passim*).[3] Not to put too fine a point on it, although initiations do have important cognitive effects, it does not seem that initiates ever *know* anything more than the others (Richards 1956: 126).

Initiation rites thus display what may be called a cognitive paradox. A common feature of initiation operations is their obscurity; they are difficult to describe as anything but gratuitous vexations and the solemn imposition of a vacuous 'knowledge'. It is quite common that initiates have nothing much to say about what they had to go through, not just because it is forbidden to communicate those secrets, but also because their memories of the rite do not constitute any significant description. Thus, a change which is most often expressed in cognitive terms is brought about by procedures which seem either impossible to describe or too trivial to mention. What is difficult is to bring together both aspects of initiation rites, the supposed

95

effects and the procedures. It may seem possible to bridge the gap by refining our idea of the kind of knowledge acquired in such contexts; this is the main point put forward by J. La Fontaine for instance (1977: *passim*; 1985: 141–61), following whom it is an oversimplification to reduce initiation 'knowledge' to information transmitted. In the 'tribal' rituals of the Gisu of West Africa, what seem to be transmitted are skills of various kinds rather than knowledge properly speaking. The difference between initiates and neophytes is commonly expressed in terms of behaviour; the latter have supposedly acquired a certain 'know-how' as regards the relationships with ancestors or the management of social intercourse. Obviously, such a competence could not be easily reduced to explicit 'lessons' and the transmission of information; they rather imply an apprenticeship based on example and imitation. Initiation does not bring new 'ideas' but the mastery of new procedures.

However pertinent in the ethnographic context considered, these ideas cannot really solve the paradox mentioned above, for they imply a somewhat distorted view of those two aspects whose combination is problematic. That initiations can confer some kind of 'know how' is certainly true; however, it remains that in the groups concerned, the difference is expressed in terms of secret *knowledge* and implies that the initiates' utterances on certain domains are true. And the problem remains, as concerns the procedures; even if we admitted that initiations transmitted some 'competence', the type of procedures used would remain quite puzzling. Competence can surely be transmitted through example and imitation, but initiation ordeals are precisely difficult to describe as meaningful 'examples' of anything, and very often there is no relationship at all between what is experienced during the ritual and the type of competent behaviour expected afterwards.

Let me illustrate these points with an extreme case, that of male initiation among the Beti of Cameroon; the rite is mentioned by many ethnographers in the area because of its outstanding complexity and symbolic elaboration (see Houseman 1984, 1986). It involves several months of secluded life in bush camps, with a complicated series of ordeals, the main feature of which is a combination of logical quandaries and humiliation or physical violence. Most of the ordeals could be described as the enactment of a conceptual antinomy. Thus, the candidates are told to go hunting some invisible animals in the bush, and find themselves hunted and attacked by the elders. They are told about the delicious fat of the antelope (*soo*), a delicacy they will be given at a crucial point in the ritual; and in fact they are force-fed a disgusting mixture of rotten food, excrement and semen. They are told they will learn how to forge iron, and consequently must 'practice', which in fact means having their fingers crushed between heavy logs. In much the same way, 'blowing the initiation horn' actually means being forced to blow in the master's anus, 'being allowed to wash' means being forced to roll on thorny bushes, and so on (Houseman 1984, 1986). Most Beti men have gone through these ordeals, and anyone who has failed them would find it impossible to hold any office or have any position other than that of a social minor. The lack of a parallel institution is the official reason of women's alleged inability to take any important decisions or indeed make any definite and important statement about things that matter, such as marriage, witchcraft, or village politics.

The Beti example provides a dramatic illustration of the cognitive paradox of initiations. While the ordeals are incomprehensible (and unpleasantly so) the resulting 'competence' is maximal, and confers the capacity of saying the truth on most domains of reality. In some traditional initiations the contrast is not so evident, but the problem remains, that initiations are defined as rituals which, among other things, allow some people to make true statements about certain matters. The actors concerned seldom explain how going through a humiliating ordeal should make one more 'competent'; this is why anthropological studies tend to play down the problem, or reduce it to the construction of an impressive decorum. But this implies a massive distortion of the ethnographical facts. All the groups concerned emphasise that the ordeals are a condition of competence *sine qua non*. As La Fontaine points out, this is taken as an axiom. Our task then should be to explain how this axiom can be taken as convincing or inescapable.

Initiations and causal interpretation

In the common implicit view of traditional truth, members of the groups concerned are supposed to think that the initiates have a 'correct' picture of the world, which is communicated in their utterances; and this is why the utterances are taken to be true. As this view of initiation truth leads to the paradox mentioned above, we must examine whether a causal account would fare better. In such a framework, the initiates' utterance would be considered true by the listeners insofar as they can represent some causal link between certain domains of reality and the utterances made about them. Initiation rituals would then be situations whose representation allows people to represent such a causal link.

This account seems to follow very closely the very interpretation the actors usually give of their initiation rituals. Let us consider for instance the case of the Mianmin initiations described by D. S. Gardner (1983). The successive stages of rituals establish the formal distinction between *diil* and *duwaiin*, those who know and those who don't. The rituals include the presentation of ancestral relics (skulls and trophies) as well as the revelation of the secret names of plants, animals and artefacts. Neophytes are also taught secret songs, generally of a mythical character. In short, everything here seems to be expressed in terms of information communicated. However, Gardner points out that such a description must be qualified, as 'rituals are considered efficient regardless of what can be called the cognitive change brought about in the candidates' (1983: 352). The rituals are successfully accomplished, even if the candidates have not understood anything in the initiatic teaching. When the relics are exposed, it is not compulsory to look at them. As for the secret names of things, one is allowed not to hear or memorise them; this does not affect the general result of the ritual. Not to put too fine a point on it, the crucial element in the ritual is not the transmission of information about the ancestors, but the fact that the candidates have been 'exposed' to the power or influence of the ancestors. This 'exposure' is what makes the difference between *diil* and *duwaiin* (1983: 339); this is why the initiatic process is viewed as a causal one, which brings about changes in people by following some recipe, even if people have no idea how the process actually works (1983: 353).

This I think is not an exceptional example; in most initiations, the fact that information is not properly communicated does not in any sense hinder the ritual process. Indeed, in many cases the candidates actually avoid receiving any information at all, e.g., in the Bambara *komo*-brotherhood rituals in Mali, in which most neophytes stop their ears when being told the potentially harmful 'secrets' of the brotherhood (Dieterlen and Cissé 1972: 80). In the Baktaman rituals described by F. Barth, the candidates develop an 'epistemology of secrecy', the main principle of which is that ritual knowledge is dangerous, so that it is safer to avoid it as much as possible (Barth 1975: 218ff.). What is always assumed and proclaimed in such contexts is that there is a necessary link between the ritual process itself and the veracity of subsequent assertions; being initiated is a prerequisite of truthful discourse. This idea of a necessary condition is puzzling if we assume that people evaluate the initiates' assertions in a 'descriptive' way. If utterances are judged solely on their content, then whether they were acquired in a specific context or not should not change their value. The fact that they were acquired in paradoxical, unintelligible ordeals should not add to their reliability, quite the contrary. As we saw in other domains, however, criteria of truth are not necessarily founded on such a 'descriptive' evaluation. Like any form of representation, utterances can be judged on their causal links to the situations they describe, i.e., as consequences or indices of these situations. This seems to be the case for the criteria applied to many traditional statements. Instead of being judged only on their content, utterances are also considered as events which, like any other type of events, have causes and consequences. This makes it possible to consider the statement about a certain state of affairs as a consequence of that state of affairs.

I would argue that it is possible, in this 'causal' framework, to solve the cognitive paradox of initiations. In this view, what the initiates assert about, say, ancestors would be represented as something caused by the ancestors themselves. The features of initiations we considered here precisely suggest that one of the aims is to make it possible for hidden entities and agencies to have some direct effects on the neophytes. I would therefore argue that, if initiation rites are conceived by the actors as consisting in such contacts and direct encounters, they make hypotheses about subsequent discourse as triggered by these agencies much more salient. Initiation rites, among other things, make it possible to represent the initiates as persons under direct influence, therefore as persons whose utterances are more likely to be caused by the agencies, entities or states of affairs they make statements about.

In the light of this hypothesis, the main features of initiation rites become much less puzzling and paradoxical. The fact that the information conveyed during the rites is virtually vacuous, and that the candidates can avoid the teaching and still be considered initiates, all this is difficult to understand in a 'descriptive' account. If we admit that people use causal criteria, on the other hand, the transmission of information clearly becomes secondary. What makes initiates more 'truthful' than ordinary speakers is a series of events, in which they are put in direct contact with hidden agencies or entities. Clearly, if this is the point of the rite, the acquisition of information is irrelevant, or else is considered as a mere side-effect of the direct contact established. Obviously, this is not all there is to say about initiation rites and their recurrent features, notably paradoxical or impossible ordeals, the use of empty secrets and physical violence.[4] Our problem here, however, is not to account for these striking features, but to understand how they can be conceived as a prerequisite for truthful discourse. A general account of initiation rites and their cognitive effects would certainly require more refined descriptions and hypotheses; but I would claim that, inasmuch as it deals with initiation as a condition of truth, it would have to take into account the fact that the initiates' utterances are judged on the basis of causal criteria.

Competence and position

A consequence of our causal account is to change drastically the idea of 'competence' or 'knowledge' involved in such statements. It is always tempting to view traditional specialists as the equivalent of experts in complex societies, i.e., people especially competent in some domain. However, the ordinary idea of competence implies that some people have acquired an accurate representation of a certain domain of reality, so that their utterances describe what the domain really is. The idea that someone is competent about Italy because they have travelled there extensively rests on the assumption that travelling there has given them an accurate representation of the country. Contrast this with the case of utterances judged on the basis of causal criteria. What is established as a link between the realities described and the utterance; as a consequence, the representations which make the idea of this link more salient are bound to be used as criteria of truth. The 'customisation' of speech provides such representations, and so does the customisation of persons which initiation rites purport to accomplish. Divination in itself is not a guarantee of veracity, no more than initiation rites in themselves make people truthful. The point is that such elements can become criteria of truth only if the listeners have specific assumptions about the way the utterances are produced, e.g., the idea that utterances are directly caused by the situations at hand. In such cases, the fact that the experts have an accurate representation of the world is by-passed, as I said above. Situations cause utterances by speaking for themselves, as it were. If this is the way the listeners interpret a series of utterances, then the representations stored in the experts' minds are not supposed to play any role in the production of utterances. This, in fact, is what many speakers in traditional contexts forcefully argue, by claiming that their utterances are 'inherited' or 'inspired', i.e., not a consequence of their own knowledge or communicative intentions.

The idea of traditional 'competence', as found in anthropological descriptions, is inadequate to describe such processes; its main flaw is that it is ambiguous. If the claim is taken in a strong way, to imply that traditional experts derive the utterances they make from general knowledge of a 'theoretical' nature about the topics treated, then it is clearly false; the rituals which are supposed to convey this knowledge turn out to be vacuous, the secrets are empty. If, on the other hand, the idea of 'competence' only implies that experts know the precise words of the myth or the gestures of the ritual, then it is certainly true but is not sufficient in order to explain why the utterances should be considered true. In the causal account I have put forward, there is no need to suppose that the listeners interpret the veracity of the utterances as an effect of the speaker's knowledge. An utterance is judged true, not because the speaker has the appropriate picture of the world in his or her mind, but because a causal link is assumed to exist between the state of affairs described and the event of the person making the utterance.

If we accept this interpretation, then we must have some precise hypotheses about the way social positions are represented in traditional interaction. We are claiming that people represent a link between a state of affairs and the utterance about it. But if only certain persons are supposed to make true statements, then it should imply that only these persons are considered liable to be involved in such causal processes. To take a simple example, the audience consider that shamans speak the truth about spirits because the spirit-situation, as it were, speaks through them; but the audience also thinks that *only* shamans say the truth about spirits. It follows that there must be some representations which make it possible to think that only shamans can be involved in the causal process in question. These persons are different;

rather, people have some representations about their being different, which account for the fact that only they can have situations speak through them. What are these representations?

Traditional positions, i.e., positions as implied in traditional interaction, are usually taken as a subset in the larger domain of social statuses, defined by specific combinations of rights and duties.[5] The problem with this approach is that it deals with an objective evaluation; it is very unlikely that social positions are *represented* in that way. Among the Fang, positions such as 'ngengang' (healer) or 'mbommvet' (epic singer) are more than 'complexes of roles' objectively defined in terms of rights and duties, because they are *named*; it is the underlying mental processes of categorisation that we must explain here.

Terms used to denote social positions are usually characterised by the fact that the persons to whom they apply perform certain activities. If there was a systematic link between category membership and activities, it would be possible to consider traditional positions as some kind of system. However, the link is not systematic at all. There is not only a problem about some activities being shared between several positions and *vice versa* (this would not necessarily compromise the idea of a system or of structured semantic domains); a more difficult problem concerns the very nature of the link. The idea of a definition implies that the activities constitute a list of conditions for membership in the category concerned.[6] In the following sections I will examine whether the occupations used to characterise positions are necessary or sufficient, and then draw some conclusions about the way positions and persons are represented in traditional contexts.

Positions and their 'definition'

Let me first consider the question whether the occupation cited as the characteristic of a class of people is a necessary feature of that class. Let us take the example of the 'castes' of craftsmen that can be found in most West African societies. The usual pattern is that of a small group of people who undertake all non-agricultural activities (blacksmithing, pottery, weaving, medicine, etc.) opposed to a vast majority of agriculturalists. The craftsmen are generally deemed 'inferior', 'polluting' and isolated from the rest of the group by a strict endogamy (Clement 1948, Maret 1980).[7] There is a complex symbolic elaboration about the exclusion and impurity of these people, and their activities are central in these reasonings. The Mafa of Cameroon for instance have a caste called *ngwalda*; these are the group's blacksmiths, potters, healers, undertakers and diviners. The exclusion of these people is justified by the fact that they manipulate such dangerous things as iron-ore and fire, that they handle polluting objects like corpses, that they bake pieces of earth (pots) rather than planting things in the earth to 'be baked' (i.e., to grow) there. In other words, the position of ngwalda is invariably explained and justified in terms of the activities performed (Martin 1970, Genest 1976). The actual performance of these activities, however, is not a necessary condition; most ngwaldas and ngwalda-lineages have nothing to do with iron-smelting, some have never acted as undertakers, etc.; but the idea that the ritual exclusions should not apply to these people would seem incongruous. One is born a member of that group and stays so whatever activities one performs. In other words, the activities are mentioned as an *a posteriori* explanation of the exclusion, not as a necessary condition for being a ngwalda. This idea is suggested by the circular explanations that can be found in Mafa myths. Some of these stories say that ngwaldas were given the dangerous job of undertakers because they were 'strong' enough to handle furnaces, or alternatively that they had to accept a dangerous activity like blacksmithing because they were too 'weak' to resist, being polluted by corpse-handling (Martin 1970: 34ff., Genest 1976: 23).[8] Not to put too fine a point on it, even when some activities are clearly designated as the exclusive lot of a certain category, the activities are not taken as a *necessary* condition for membership of the category (Boyer 1982b *passim*).

Conversely, it is often clear that the activity mentioned as a 'definition' of the position is a *non-sufficient* condition, so that one can have the occupation without the position. This is precisely what happens with the Fang positions mentioned above, and it applies to most positions linked to ritual activities and more generally to the handling of traditional truths. A Fang mbommvet can be defined as someone who plays the mvet instrument and knows the repertoire of epic tales. However, many people who fulfill such criteria are not considered mbommvet at all. This concerns not only young inexperienced story-tellers but also musicians coming from distant clans; and it happens that some persons, formerly said to be mvet players, are not so considered any longer. All this means that membership of the category mbommvet can be the subject of conjectures beyond such obvious properties as playing the instrument and knowing the stories.

In most cases of traditional positions, activities are only *part* of what is required; one has to have 'something more' that marks the 'true' or 'real' holders of such positions. This 'something more' is usually not defined; the Fang express it in terms of having 'eaten the medicine' (i.e., undergone the specific initiation) for this or that activity. This is very vague, and most people have no idea at all how one could 'eat' this 'medicine' or what it consists of. This in fact suggests that the persons considered are different from ordinary people in that they are evur-bearers. The idea of a 'hidden' property that explains why some mvet-playing persons are not mbommvet, means that the typical activity, however central, is not a sufficient argument for ascribing someone a categorical status; this conclusion I think applies to most traditional positions.

The idea that traditional positions are classified in terms of activities contains some truth, in that occupations are the idiom in which ideas about positions are usually expressed. However, the representation of activities cannot be the mental definition of the positions, since it provides neither necessary nor sufficient conditions for membership of the category. It is sometimes assumed that such phenomena (people performing the activities without having the position, or conversely) are just exceptions in the otherwise smooth operation of the social system. People, however, do not think of these cases as exceptions in a system of rules; they do not consider non-blacksmithing blacksmiths as being outside of the system; such persons are fully-fledged blacksmiths like the others, in much the same way as an orange-coloured lemon is strange but is still a lemon, neither an orange nor a 'half-lemon'. I think this allows us to draw some conclusions about the way people represent the link between activity and category; these conclusions apply not only to the so-called exceptions but also to cases where the activities expected are effectively performed.

As I pointed out above, we are dealing here with named positions, i.e., with a set of categories. The problem is what makes it possible to decide that a certain person is an exemplar of the category. The activities usually linked with a certain position can be described as a typical identification of the category. The important point here is the idea of typicality, i.e., of using criteria which allow one to recognise most exemplars of a category, but are insufficient to determine the extension of the term. When asked what a mbommvet is, Fang people almost always answer that it is someone who plays the mvet. When reminded that so and so plays the mvet and is not considered a mbommvet, they typically answer 'that's true, but you see that's because *he isn't* a mbommvet'. What is clearly implied by the use of the category mbommvet is that the people to whom the name applies are different from the rest of the Fang. In what way they are different is not considered, but what is known for sure is that they must be different, otherwise they would not be mbommvet. Not to put too fine a point on it, the representation of the position is a yes/no question: one is or is not a ngengang; people might be unsure in certain cases, but that never means that one could be 'half-ngengang' or 'mbommvet to a certain extent'. What makes one a mbommvet or ngengang, however, is not such observable features as playing an instrument or organizing certain rituals. It is something more that all members of those categories have. No one knows what it consists of, but it has to be there, otherwise, whatever one's activities, one is not an exemplar of the category. External typical criteria are just indirect (and insufficient) evidence of the fact that people really belong to the category.

Living kinds and naturalised positions

This type of identification makes some position terms very similar to natural kind terms, especially to the terms used to refer to living species. As I said in chapter 2, there cannot be a definition for such terms as 'giraffe' or 'oak'. The representation and use of a natural kind term always involves two types of general assumptions:

(i) some assumptions about the *typical features* of the exemplars of the kind. Although most of these features are present in most exemplars, they are neither necessary nor sufficient conditions. Thus, giraffes are supposed to be long-necked and lemons yellow. But short-necked giraffes and blueish lemons are still giraffes and lemons, so the features are not necessary. They only provide a 'stereotype' of the kind, which can be represented in various ways (as a series of features, or with the help of mental images, etc.) but never constitutes a definition. The use of a natural kind term, however, requires another general assumption.

(ii) the presumption of an *underlying trait* that is common to all exemplars of the kind. This is what makes giraffes giraffes and dogs dogs; this essential feature is necessary to the use of natural kind terms. Using the term 'giraffe' implies that beyond surface resemblance, there is something common to all real giraffes, although what this common trait consists of is left undefined.[9]

There is good psychological evidence that both types of assumption are mentally represented and govern people's use of such terms, especially in the domain of living kinds. Even in young children (four-year-olds), the presumption that living kinds have a common essence is so strong that it overrides perceptual resemblance. Children extend inductive generalisations about an exemplar to other exemplars of the same kind, even if they look very different, but never to exemplars of another kind even if they are very similar (Gelman and Markman 1987, Gelman 1988).[10] The idea of an undefined common essence is a powerful cognitive mechanism, universally available to human minds; together with basic principles of taxonomic ordering, it organises biological knowledge in all cultures (Berlin *et al.* 1973).

It is difficult not to notice the structural similarity between the representation of such categories and that of the social positions considered here. As I mentioned above, the positions involved in traditional interaction seemed to be related to characteristics such as occupation but the latter do not constitute necessary and sufficient conditions for membership. At the same time, however, people suppose that there is some underlying feature that is common to all persons in the position. In other words, there is a presumption that persons occupying a certain position share an essence, although what the essence consists of is left undefined. In many anthropological accounts, this is considered a puzzling feature. If people are given a certain position, there should be a mental 'definition' of what makes them different from others. This paradox is eliminated if we admit that positions in such a context are represented in the same way as living kinds. People who are 'mbommvet' or 'ngengang' are thus considered naturally different from others. If this difference is represented in terms of natural kinds, there is no need of a defining feature; what is necessary is just the presumption that the essential trait exists, not any hypothesis about what it consists of. Also, this hypothesis makes it possible to account for the 'exceptions' mentioned above. People who are said to belong to a caste of blacksmiths but never smelt iron are represented in the same way as short-necked giraffes, i.e., as potentially interesting cases but not as non-giraffes. A being is or is not a giraffe; there is no way of being 'half a giraffe' or 'a giraffe to a certain degree'. Although it may be difficult to identify a concrete exemplar, there is no doubt that it either belongs or does not belong to the kind.

The representation of social positions then relies on the extension to social differences of spontaneous assumptions which prove extremely successful in dealing with the natural world.[11] This of course applies *a fortiori* to social categories which are *explicitly* defined as quasi-biological species. The most salient illustration of this is the Indian *jati* which can be glossed as 'caste' in the social domain and 'species' in the natural domain, but there are countless other examples. The assumptions of shared essence and typical features seem to be a direct translation, in the domain of traditional interaction, of the way everyone from early childhood identifies and classifies natural kinds.

Position and truth

Let me now return to the general question of position and truth. Truth seems a privilege of certain social positions. Only some actors in traditional interaction are supposed to make true statements about certain domains of reality. This is difficult to understand if we maintain that traditional statements are judged on the basis of the 'competence' involved. In such a framework, initiation for instance is just incomprehensible. If, however, we assume that statements are judged on the basis of causal criteria, then it is possible to interpret such institutions as a way of establishing the causal connections deemed necessary, or more precisely as a way of making the assumption of such causal links more salient in the listeners' minds. But this in return makes it necessary to explain why only certain persons should be liable to get involved in these causal processes. My claim is that the only way of making this assumption is to represent a natural difference between people occupying certain positions and the others. This in fact is a very common strategy in both science and common sense: differences in causal power are related to underlying differences in kind. If two animals which apparently belong to the same species turn out to breed in significantly different ways, it is obviously relevant to assume that they in fact belong to different species, that the underlying traits are different.

We can now understand the apparent strength and fatal flaws of the ordinary authoritarian description of tradition. The basic insight, which relates truth to position, is right and faithful to what the actors themselves report. The conception is wrong, however, as concerns the representation of positions, which is not only a question of classification or ranking, but presupposes the attribution of a hidden, inscrutable essence to the holders of certain positions. Only some people are liable to be affected by a certain causal process: this idea presupposes an essential difference between the people concerned. Indeed such differences are very often expressed as differences between species of people, formally comparable to animal species, and justified in terms of biological differences.

Finally, let me mention a possible misunderstanding that should be avoided. This hypothesis of course does not explain why there are social positions, not even why there are certain positions and not others, even less why specific people occupy the positions. What it explains, on the other hand, is why and how, once the positions exist, it is possible for people to take them as a criterion of truth. This, as I said, is impossible to understand if we maintain that positions are mentally defined or that utterances are judged are the expression of some 'competence'. The connection between veracity and specific positions is plausible only if the categories in question are represented in the same way as living kinds, if the positions are naturalised.

7

Conclusions and programme

In the course of this book I have left aside some problems which are usually considered crucial in a characterisation of tradition, concerning, e.g. the classical opposition of 'tradition' and 'modernity', the question of 'traditional societies' and of a 'traditional mentality', the problem of the relationship between literacy and oral traditions, etc. Although these problems should all be dealt with in a theory of tradition, it is difficult to go beyond common platitudes if we do not have a precise description of traditional interaction itself. In this chapter I will try to re-examine these questions in the light of the hypotheses put forward about the intellectual processes involved in traditional discourse. I will start with a general picture of the theory so far, then examine some of its possible implications, and finally suggest some directions for further research.

We examined here a limited domain of traditional interaction, namely the cognitive processes involved in traditional discourse. This way of approaching the subject is not meant to suggest that traditions are just series of statements. Obviously, many aspects of traditional situations are non-verbal; these elements are remembered and repeated and constitute traditional objects, often but not always in combination with verbal communication. In presenting a mainly 'verbal' account of traditions, I do not mean to imply that non-discursive aspects are secondary; my reason for choosing to focus on utterances was mainly tactical. In the common anthropological views, traditions are described as founded on some set of conserved underlying propositions about the world. If this were the case, the analysis of traditional utterances should not pose too many difficult problems. Obviously, language is the richest representative idiom in which propositions, 'theories', 'world-views' and 'conceptions' could be expressed, much more easily than in dance, ritual gestures, pictorial representations, etc. In other words, if traditions were about world-views, the study of traditional discourse should have no difficulty in uncovering them.

It turns out, however, that traditional utterances cannot really be linked to underlying conceptions without systematically distorting the data, overlooking many of their important properties or creating difficult problems. True, the different types of traditional discourse I have examined *could* be described in terms of world-views transmitted, but at the price of focusing on irrelevant aspects and leaving aside the crucial features of each type of discourse. For instance, traditional truths in certain societies must be expressed in a ritual language whose structure minimizes the 'meanings' conveyed. One could still claim that some 'meanings' are transmitted despite the ritual language. But what then is the point of conveying them in an obscure, misleading form? One would have to interpret this as some form of 'noise' in the communication of world-views. As it happens, however, the people concerned take the formalisation of speech to be, not a contextual or secondary property, but a crucial feature, so much so that a translation in ordinary language is not supposed to convey a truth at all. By taking the expression or transmission of information as the main point of the ritual, we would both create a difficult problem (why do people bother to use complicated verbal forms?) and consider irrelevant what the actors take to be essential, what they often try to transmit from generation to generation. As we have seen, the same point can be made about divination or initiation rites as the origin of true discourse.

This has some consequences in the study of traditions in general. If traditional statements do not convey a world-view, then other aspects of traditions (gestures, dance, and other types of action) must be *a fortiori* even less 'expressive' in that sense. The actual study of traditions, as complex phenomena of memorisation which integrate specific gestures and actions as well as utterances, has not yet been undertaken in anthropology; but one point at least is clear: such a study cannot start from the assumption that the expression of underlying theories or conceptions is the principal aspect of traditional actions.

Traditions and psychological hypotheses

Theories of tradition necessarily imply some claims about mental representations and processes. Reiterated phenomena could not be reiterated without people memorising them; salient actions are salient only if people's attention is mobilised by them; literalism is a psychological attitude toward variations at the 'surface' of the cultural phenomena considered. As I pointed out in the foreword, it is difficult to put forward a plausible theory of tradition without having some clear psychological assumptions. This applies to common accounts of traditional interaction too: terms such as 'conservatism' or 'traditionalism' refer to cognitive and emotive states, processes and mechanisms.

The processes described in the previous chapters are for the most part simple and common properties of people's reasonings. Three features appear to be particularly important in the interpretation of traditional contexts.

(i) *Causal criteria of truth.* The listeners judge a certain utterance true because they represent the existence of a causal link between a current state of affairs and the event of the utterance about it. This of course is an abstract analytical description. People do not have to represent such logical terms as 'causal links', 'states of affairs', etc., to represent a singular causal interpretation of an event, e.g. an utterance. People's criteria of truth are always expressed in the concrete terms; a specific state of affairs causes a specific event, in this case a singular utterance.

(ii) *Anchored categories.* This refers to the process whereby a notion is stripped down of its general definitional features. Some traditional notions have no definitional features at all and others are *prima facie* 'normal' or definable notions, about which it is then assumed that the accepted definitional features are insufficient for a really referential use of the term. The distinction between common use and truth-making registers is essential. The acquisition of expert discourse implies, not the acquisition of new general representations about the entities designated, but the memorisation of ostensive presentations of these entities or properties.

(iii) *Naturalised positions.* This is another aspect which is often mentioned in anthropological texts, although its relevance for a general theory of traditions is not clearly perceived. Positions are conceived in terms of essence, in much the same way as living kinds. The accession to a certain position is therefore conceived as the unfolding of underlying properties rather than as a contingent change in people's activities, even when such a change is the only means to recognize the position. The representation of positions as natural makes it possible to conceive certain causal links as affecting certain persons only.

The original feature, the characteristic of traditions, is the *combination* of these processes. This combination is found in situations where claims are made about the truth of certain statements, and about the efficacy of certain recipes for producing truths. This process obviously involves not only a certain organisation of the utterances, but also a certain type of cooperation on the part of the addressees, and some specific ways of memorising such situations. In other words, tradition is conceived here as a specific type of *communication*, not in the restricted sense of a transmission of information, but rather as a type of interaction which modifies people's representations in a relatively organised way.

These three hypotheses are no doubt insufficient to constitute a complete theory of traditions; there may be other essential features of this type of cultural institution, and the features mentioned here perhaps deserves a more refined psychological description. The hypotheses, however, make it possible to account for some of the general properties with which anthropologists are familiar, yet are seldom taken into account in theories. Among such properties are the criteria of traditional style I mentioned in chapter 1, namely the fact that people's attention is focused on singular events rather than general principles, the consequent literalism and the fact that some institutions are supposedly justified by the fact that they have been done before in much the same way. Common conceptions of tradition have little to say about these common properties. They cannot account for the insistence on singular instances, which is virtually denied in intellectualist models: people are supposed to think in theoretical terms, although they are constantly talking about singular cases. As for literalism, it is interpreted as a consequence of people's traditionalism, but this is certainly no explanation; the idea of a spontaneous conservatism is too vague to be of any explanatory value. The fact that repetition is a sufficient justification for performing certain actions receives no explanation at all. A theory of tradition should certainly be judged on the type of account it gives for such general properties; the cognitive hypotheses put forward here were chosen precisely because they make it possible to account for these common aspects of traditional institutions.

Implications (1): traditions and societies

In the course of this argument I have described traditions without mentioning the anthropological and philosophical debates about the 'Great Divide' between 'tradition' and 'modernity', these being understood as different types of societies or different mentalities. The societies generally considered 'traditional' in anthropological dichotomies can be roughly described as exotic, small-scale peasant or pastoral communities. The Fang, Beti, Cuna, Mianmin, Mundang, etc., from whose institutions I drew my examples and illustrations, live in such groups. So do most of the people classical anthropological monographs are about. There is therefore a strong tendency in anthropology to think that generalities about traditions are necessarily generalities about this type of societies, as opposed to large empires or kingdoms, modern industrial nations or ancient city-states.

In the conception proposed here, the question may be raised, whether the type of interaction I have described as the foundation of traditional repetition can be found only in a certain type of society. 'Great Divide' models just beg these questions, since concepts such as 'traditional mentality' or 'traditional society' are the starting point of the theoretical constructions. This of course is an empirical question, not a matter of *a priori* judgement. I have mainly described traditions in terms of processes of representations and communication, which may be typical of a certain type of social environment, or not. I will argue that the latter is more likely, in other words that traditions can be found in very diverse types of societies, although we must be wary of some conceptual confusions about this question.

This position may seem odd, since all the examples I have mentioned in the course of this book were taken from societies which would fall on the 'traditional' side of any 'Great Divide' conception. The reason for this is not that examples could not be found elsewhere, but a simpler point of method. If we want to uncover some general properties of tradition, it is certainly safer, and I hope more convincing, to take as a starting point institutions which are uncontroversial examples of 'traditions' in the usual sense. At the same time however, most of the phenomena I have described here must have a familiar ring to anthropologists who have worked in those supposedly 'non-traditional' environments. Divination is rife in industrial societies (and probably widespread in all civilisations); so is the idea that specific individuals have a particular relationship to hidden entities or agencies, which allows them to state the truth about certain domains of experience. To take a more trivial example, it is difficult for an anthropologist to describe the 'bullying' to which neophytes are subjected in many modern institutions, notably the armies, as anything but a form of initiation. Does this mean that what I have proposed here as the general properties of traditions can be found in most, maybe all societies? My answer (necessarily a tentative one since this is an empirical question) is that traditional interaction can indeed be found in other societies than prototypical small exotic communities; to which I hasten to add the reservation, that mere similarities of institutions (such as in the examples above) are certainly not sufficient to infer that one is dealing with a traditional interaction, with all the properties described here. To substantiate what may seem a Byzantine qualification, I will give two opposite examples of modern institutions, which seem to me clear cases of non-traditional and traditional interaction respectively.

The first example concerns 'experts' in modern industrial societies, e.g., specialists of computers or of the economy, who are treated with implicit confidence as sources of truth about certain domains of reality by a 'general public' who have no means to assess the validity of their arguments in any detail. This situation may appear, and is often described as, similar to that of the traditional specialists I have described here. The representations involved, however, are very different, and the resemblance is only a superficial one. The very idea of *competence* implies that such experts have in their minds an adequate description of the domain of reality concerned, e.g., the workings of the economy or of the human body. They are also supposed to develop an expert 'hunch', a capacity for inferring complex underlying mechanisms from apparently trivial indices. Such skills are conceived as rooted in learning and practice; the assumption is that the combination of abstract knowledge and past experience has given these people a view of these domains which corresponds to the reality.

The picture is very different in the case of traditional specialists. If my hypotheses are correct, then the very idea of 'competence' as described above is irrelevant. In certain people's utterances, truths are expressed because these utterances are made in such situations that they are constrained and provoked by the realities themselves. The speaker's representations are, as I said in chapter 5, entirely by-passed. Elders who talk on behalf of the ancestors are in fact letting the ancestors talk through them, and the idea of real states of affairs directly influencing a statement is fundamental in divination rituals too. In other words, a traditional specialist is not someone who has an adequate picture of some reality in her or his mind, but someone whose utterances can be, in some contexts, directly determined by the reality in question. This crucial difference also explains why expert statements and the reproduction of expert knowledge are not at all comparable with ritualised statements or initiation processes. The fact that people trust experts implicitly in modern industrial societies does not imply that the criteria of truth and the process of legitimation are the same.

A strikingly different situation is that of the London 'witches' described in T. Luhrmann's monograph and articles (1986). These, I hasten to say, are not members of a bizarre sect in search of ecstatic experience. Most of them are sober and rational people, who use the various resources of European or other folklore to create situations in which the interplay of ritual action and free imaginative associations makes it possible to experience 'another level of reality', and supposedly to have access to truths beyond the reach of everyday cognition. Their view of the effects of magic is rather pedestrian, based on a rather empiricist idea of trial and error rather than 'mystical' adherence to a creed. The interaction that takes place in these 'covens' can certainly be described as traditional, in the sense that it displays all the features I have described above. The crucial notions are ordinary terms made undefinable. The specific rhetoric of magical discourse aims at depriving common words of their ordinary reference, so that the 'forces' and other elements of magical action are considered beyond definition or description. Acquiring these notions means diverging from their everyday understanding and going through a series of situations which constitute ostensive presentations, e.g. of the magical 'force' or 'power'. Each group is led by an 'adept', whose utterances are supposed to convey important truths about the hidden forces and agencies. The 'adept' has a special access to these forces, and is described as being put under 'pressure' or being 'pushed' by them. The guarantee that these persons make true statements is therefore to be found in the fact that their utterances are caused by the forces they are talking about. To the participants in the ritual, there is an undefined state of the forces which causes the adept's utterances. Thus, the pattern of interaction between members of the 'covens' has all the features of traditional communication. And one of the results of this communicative interaction is the repetition or reiteration of specific ritual situations.

My aim in making these remarks is not to deny the obvious differences between groups like the Fang and other societies, with a strikingly different social organisation and intellectual climate, but to replace these differences in a broader context, that of the multiplicity of claims to truth made in any society at any period. In the previous chapters I mentioned the Fang tradition of epic singing, their divinatory traditions and the tradition of ancestor-cult. There is no unique access to knowledge, but rather a variety of institutions concerned with different domains of reality. Furthermore, in a Fang village people make many claims to truth, which are not linked to a traditional situation in any sense. Competent drivers or people who know about distant regions of Cameroon are just supposed to have acquired the right skills and representations from the accumulation of relevant experience or from some appropriate tuition, and nothing more. This in fact applies to most domains of everyday activities.

What makes the Fang intellectual climate evidently different from that, say of the Chinese empire, Greek city-states or suburban London is the fact that most, in fact nearly all salient, socially significant and memorable claims to truth are made in the context of traditional interaction. These claims to truth are founded on the idea of a causal link between states of affairs and utterances about them; they imply a naturalised representation of people's positions and the episodic 'anchoring' of certain crucial notions. In short, most truths beyond the sphere of common sense are stated in traditional situations. The difference between this, and a society where a significant number of socially salient claims to truth are made in non-traditional settings and interactions, might well be one of degree and not of nature. Obviously, there may be a difference in nature between these types of societies. I am only claiming that there is no corresponding divide, in ways of defending the veracity of certain statements.

These empirical arguments make it possible to understand more precisely why Great Divide models are an obstacle rather than a springboard for theories of traditional interaction. Most of these models pose difficult problems, notably the following:

(i) in most formulations, 'tradition' and 'modernity' are treated as essences. It is assumed that there are two *kinds* of societies or cultures. Obviously, this is question-begging; the question, whether societies where traditional interaction is observed constitute a different kind, is an empirical question. It cannot be solved *a priori*, but only in the light of data and theories;

(ii) the distinctions are asymmetrical. As Gellner points out (1974: 150), the distinction is made, either between the domain of 'tradition' and an ill-defined variety of non-traditional societies, or conversely between a precisely defined type of rational thinking and some vague idea of tradition. In the latter case, tradition is a residual category, which lumps together Pygmy hunters and Chinese mandarins, Zande herdsmen and

Hindu priests. The fact that this set is rather disparate, to put things mildly, is obscured by the assumption that all these people are 'traditionalistic', again a supposedly unproblematic description;

(iii) this unbalanced description leads authors to focus on the question of the demise of tradition and the birth of a modern, scientifically oriented culture. This relies on the assumption that people are naturally 'traditionalistic', that they normally stick to past generations' beliefs, until extraordinary circumstances force them to abandon that attitude. Once again, one just begs the question why and how the actors happen to find past practice convincing and sufficient.

These might be taken as accidental defects in the current formulations of the Great Divide question, but I think the flaws are in fact inherent to any such dichotomy. There is simply no reason why the properties of traditions should be amenable to a dichotomised description. Traditions are a complex form of interaction; they involve a specific distribution of roles between people, a specific type of criteria to evaluate their utterances, a specific kind of representation about certain cultural categories, and so on. As I tried to make clear in the rest of the book, the *combination* of these elements makes it possible for traditional interaction to occur and result in the repetition of communicative events. Most of the elements are likely to be found in other types of situations, perhaps even in prototypical 'modern' contexts. The reasons why simplistic dichotomies are rife in the study of traditions have more to do with an historically dated obsession with the difference between 'us' and 'them', than with any serious scientific argument.

Implications (2): tradition and literacy

I must now turn to a much more specific question, that of the relationship between the type of communicative interaction I have described here and the presence or absence of literacy. There is a vast literature on this subject, which I will survey only briefly, to indicate some consequences of the idea that traditions are not systems of ideas or conceptions but patterns of social interaction. The importance of the relationships between oral traditions and literacy has been emphasised by J. Goody in a series of papers and books (Goody and Watt 1963, Goody 1977, 1986, 1987) the main point of which was to go beyond the sterile Great Divide approaches, by focusing on actual communication processes rather than abstract characteristics of 'tradition'. The existence of literacy has profound consequences on people's represent-ations of the world and on the way they organise and communicate them; in other words, literacy does not only provide a technique of information communication and storage, it has some direct effects on the type of information people make use of. Among other things, the study of the effects of literacy makes it possible to refute some deeply entrenched anthropological beliefs; for instance, the lists and tables of binary oppositions, in which structuralist anthropology sees the hallmark of the *pensée sauvage*, are typically literate devices (Goody 1977: *passim*).

The starting point in these studies is the different properties of oral and written communication as such. Obviously, the main difference lies in the status of the message, which is externally available in written communication and can therefore be apprehended independently of the originator, while oral messages are necessarily embedded in the actual face-to-face interaction of speaker and listener(s). An important consequence is what Chafe calls 'evidentiality', the fact that in an oral message it is impossible to convey some information about a domain of reality without conveying some idea of the speaker's relationship to that knowledge (Chafe 1982). Other consequences have to do with the internal coherence of written messages, rendered easier by the fact that all parts of the message are simultaneously available, and various other stylistic differences (Chafe 1982; Tannen 1985: *passim*). Furthermore, the cognitive processes involved in understanding and memorising written and oral texts are quite different (Hildyard and Olson 1982).[1]

There is a complex relationship between these properties of oral and written communication and traditional interaction. An obvious question is whether the existence of literacy precludes the type of interaction I have described here. But we must distinguish two different problems here, that of the existence of some traditional interactions in a society, and that of the preeminence of traditional situations as the sole origin of truths beyond common sense and everyday experience. The answer to the first question is simple and empirically evident: there *are* traditional situations and interactions in many literate societies. I have mentioned the case of London covens, and most third-world societies illustrate the coexistence of traditional interaction with the gradual diffusion of literacy.

The second question is more difficult and historically more important. Can we say that the introduction of literacy automatically leads to the suppression of the preeminence of traditional sources of truth? The answer to this obviously depends on the understanding of the very vague notion of 'literacy'. One must be careful to distinguish between two different, sometimes divergent aspects of writing systems, which I would call the *data-storage* and the *frozen speech* aspects. Scripts can be used to store and retrieve data, i.e., encoded descriptions of states of affairs, and they can also be used to represent words and sentences of a natural language. The latter use is so familiar to us that it is sometimes difficult to take the other aspect into account, and realise that most scripts were either entirely designed for data storage or used largely for that purpose, to the exclusion of speech representation. For instance, most pictographic systems and mnemonic devices are clearly intended for data storage and retrieval. And many scripts, like, e.g., the ancient Mesopotamian and Mycenean syllabaries, were mainly used for book-keeping purposes, again to store data rather than freeze utterances in a natural language.[2]

The likely effects of literacy on traditional interaction certainly depend, to a large extent, on the relative importance of these two aspects in the social use of literacy. Scripts used mainly for data storage are by nature outside the domain of the legitimation of claims to truth; scripts mainly used to represent speech, on the other hand, can take over from oral communication in the expression and diffusion of arguments about such claims. Once writing is used in that domain, it is likely to lead to the demise of traditional legitimation as described here. The idea, for instance, that true utterances are speech-events directly *caused* by some real state of affairs, is clearly inapplicable to written messages, which are necessarily detached from particular speakers and circumstances.[3] Other properties of traditional interaction, such as the strict, quasi-biological identification of truthful people as directly influenced by specific states of affairs, become irrelevant too; and this can lead to extreme situations such as that of classical Greece, where very few domains of truth are beyond the written argumentation of the literate elite.[4]

Obviously, the 'frozen speech' use of literacy is a necessary but non-sufficient condition for that process. As G. Lloyd points out, the development of empirical, polemically 'anti-magical' types of argumentation in classical Greece cannot be attributed to the sole effects of literacy, which appeared more than two centuries before; moreover, the division between written and oral does not exactly map that between traditional and empirical arguments (Lloyd 1979: 227, 239ff., see also Scribner and Cole 1981). Even in Greek city-states, the intellectual climate of which was clearly 'agnostic', literate communication was not immediately used for the expression of claims to truth. One can therefore see literacy as a 'multiplier', in the economic sense, rather than the sole determinant of such processes. Casting traditionally created truths in the written format is the first step on a slippery slope that may lead to the discussion and contestation of these truths.

Truth, acquisition and salience

Let me now turn to possible further directions. I shall begin with a number of platitudes, in relation to the conclusions of chapter 2. Ideally, an anthropological theory should at least provide some means of understanding what makes certain ideas and values so natural and obvious to people living in a certain cultural environment. Explaining this is as difficult as it is necessary; not surprisingly, the problem is often ignored or treated with a good measure of handwaving. For instance, people are said to acquire by 'socialisation' the 'cultural models' and 'symbols' that give 'meaning' to various events. The explanatory power of such ideas is rather small, to put it mildly. Even if given more substance, they imply several not-too-plausible hypotheses, among which the following:

1 people live in fairly coherent cultural environments, where propositions about such things as ancestors or gods are clearly stated, neither too numerous nor too complex;
2 acquiring such ideas is a simple process. Subjects just pick up what is in the air, as it were, and use it;
3 there are no strong cognitive constraints on what cultures consist of. As long as the 'models' provide 'meaning' where needed, indefinitely variable ideas will do.

Unfortunately, each of these hypotheses just flies in the face of the facts. First and foremost, people do not live in such simple cultural environments. People have access to lots of singular actions and utterances, many of which are unrelated or inconsistent. They must build on these singular data by a process of inductive generalisation. The resulting models are not transmitted; what are transmitted, on the other hand, are specific recipes, words, gestures and other such 'surface' phenomena. Moreover, psychologists know that the acquisition of simple notions or relations is not a simple process; if acquiring the meaning of 'chair', 'uncle' and 'cause' involves complex mechanisms, this should hold *a fortiori* for concepts and propositions which are less obviously anchored in everyday experience. By and large, most cognitive psychologists agree that the only way of accounting for learning processes is to posit strong innate mechanisms, which produce inductive generalisations, make it possible to weigh their plausibility and correct them, and so on. Inevitably, this implies that there are strong constraints on 'learnability'; human subjects cannot form just any hypothesis, cannot learn just any artificial language, etc. But this of course makes claim 3 rather difficult to maintain; anything will just not do as a 'cultural model'. There are some limits to what people can acquire in order to generate 'meaning'.

Going further than these platitudes, however, is especially difficult in anthropology. It would be highly unrealistic to claim that the hypotheses made in the course of this book provide a comprehensive alternative to the inadequate 'explanations' criticised here. I would claim, however, that they make it possible to imagine some directions of research, toward a more empirically plausible account of the acquisition of cultural ideas. In order to make this rather ambitious claim less abstract, let me return to the central question of the criteria of truth used in traditional interaction. In chapters 2 to 6, I tried to show that what makes certain types of discourse 'traditional' can be described as *a specific organisation of the claims to truth*.[5] Criteria of truth are in principle as varied as utterances themselves. Most societies, however, have some institutionalised sources of true statements, with specific criteria. Certain *recipes* are supposed to result in the production of true statements; I have described traditional institutions as such recipes, positing that some interesting common properties make them different from the claims to truth which can be found in other situations.

The very notion of a *claim* to truth implies that the actors do not necessarily take to be true whatever statement is made according to the recipe. In many cases there is some competition about which recipes are the most appropriate. Even when subjects take a recipe as really effective, their commitment to the end result is extremely variable, and depends only partly on the characteristics of the recipe. This is why I tried to keep separate, in chapter 3, the public phenomenon of *truth-ascription*, about which I have put forward a specific hypothesis, and that of conviction or *adherence*, which deserves a separate study. Truth-ascription is the process whereby a selection is made, between the utterances which express a truth and those which do not. The outcome of this process is both simple (an utterance conveys some truth or not) and easily explicated. People's conviction or commitment on the other hand, their adherence to the proposition expressed by a certain sentence, is a 'private' reality. It is neither simple nor easily described; there are many shades and degrees of commitment.

In anthropological 'theories of belief', the two phenomena are usually conflated, or discussed in the same breath, which suggests that they are necessarily connected. In such a framework, people find true whatever they are convinced of, and they are convinced of whatever they say is true. The problem with this conception is that it does not provide any means to describe the varying degree of commitment to a proposition judged 'true'; this is problematic, since these nuances of commitment might be extremely relevant in the description of some traditional 'beliefs'. More precisely, judging a statement 'true' can result in a variety of attitudes, from a slightly doubtful adherence to complete, rock-bottom commitment. This cannot be described in a theory which recognises only two states, belief and unbelief, corresponding to truth and falsity.

There are no degrees of veracity, but there are degrees of adherence.[6] The fact that subjects can have a varying commitment to propositions which are all marked as 'true' is more easily understood if we take into account that criteria of truth are specific representations about an utterance, a speaker, a context, etc. More precisely, they are *assumptions* about these realities. The listener who judges that the assertion 'ant-hills indicate witchcraft' is true makes this judgement on the basis of assumptions about the speaker (he has undergone the witch-experts' initiation), the situation (the statement is made during a specific ritual), and other background factors (other statements have been made about such ant-hills, or about witchcraft being made manifest by other indices, etc.).

118

Without entering into the complex reasonings involved, we must observe that such assumptions, like all assumptions, have a variable strength or salience. To take but one aspect of this specific example, the fact that the speaker *is* a witchcraft-expert who has undergone the appropriate initiation is not a simple matter. It is an empirical assumption, which can be given more or less salience by many factors and experiences, by memories of other people's statements, by memories of the speaker's previous utterances, etc. There is simply no way of explaining why some people's utterances are received with more credence than others', if we do not consider what makes it salient that they do occupy the position in question. This is why I tried in chapters 3, 4 and 6 to debunk the common idea that people believe a certain divinatory statement because they hold a certain cultural axiom, which says that 'whatever diviners say is true'. Besides its distinct tautological aspect, this explanation is flawed in that it suggests that the identification of experts is a simple process of classification. In fact, it implies complex processes of hypothesis formation and confirmation, e.g., about the fact that the person considered possesses certain underlying features that make him or her similar to other members of the category, and about the activities as a typical feature of the category, etc.

The way inferences are influenced by the relative salience of assumptions is extremely difficult to describe, and there is no satisfactory account of these mechanisms. But the important point here is that they *do* vary in cognitive salience, and consequently in the extent to which they play a part in the process whereby an utterance is judged true. Cognitive salience is notoriously difficult to describe (and even to define precisely), but psychologists working on everyday, non-demonstrative inference and the role of background knowledge simply have to take this dimension into account.

In order to fulfil the general anthropological brief, and explain what makes it natural to take certain propositions as natural and obvious, we must therefore describe the processes whereby certain singular assumptions become more salient. This is, in essence, a question of acquisition. It may seem an impossible task: studying such 'central processes' as belief-fixation is difficult enough in psychology,[7] but the difficulty is compounded by the kind of naturalistic data anthropologists have to rely on.[8] Traditions, however, may be a privileged domain for such inquiries, in the sense that most claims to truth are associated with ritualised situations. Such 'scripted' contexts are the basis for inductive generalisations, as we saw in chapter 2. Their main characteristic is that they make use of drastically restricted recurrent material, thereby making it less tantalising to study the evolution of representations in subjects who undergo and perform such rituals. Notwithstanding the inherent difficulties of such an enterprise, the study of traditional rituals is bound to be the domain from which theories of cultural acquisition can be elaborated and tested.

Conclusion

The main question a theory of tradition should address is that of the repetition or reiteration of specific communicative situations. There is no satisfactory answer to this question in the anthropological literature, mainly because the very problem is obscured by vague notions and conceptual confusions. Instead of the repetition of concrete situations, most theories focus on an altogether different question, that of the transmission of what is vaguely described as 'conceptions' and 'world-views'. As I argued in chapter 1, such intellectual objects may well exist, but they are not of any descriptive or explanatory value in the interpretation of traditional interaction.

An empirically significant theory of tradition should explain why some specific situations acquire a special psychological salience, how they are interpreted in different ways by the different participants, and how these different processes of memorisation contribute to the reiteration or repetition of the interaction considered. In this book, obviously, I have not given such a complete theory. I have tried to give it some foundation, however, by laying stress on the cognitive processes involved in the representation of traditional contexts. Concept acquisition, the naturalisation of positions and the use of causal criteria of truth are all part of the mechanisms which contribute to the cognitive salience of certain communicative events. It remains to explain how these elements are integrated in people's representations of the events. The aim of this book was not to solve the question of traditional repetition, but to build a framework in which it is possible to address it as a significant question, as a matter for empirical investigation.

Notes

Conserved world-views of salient memories

1 Obviously, this distinction between observational and theoretical terms cannot be taken too strictly, first because 'repetition', like other empirical terms in social sciences does include some commonly agreed theoretical premises, second, because the distinction between observational and theoretical vocabularies is often problematic. The claim here is in fact rather modest, namely that the repetition of interaction is among those facts anthropology should explain, while the 'conservation of cultural models' is one of the hypotheses the discipline puts forward.

2 Holy and Stuchlik (1983) give a detailed and rigorous account of all these ambiguities, and of the possible options. I have left the question aside because it is neutral as concerns the problem at hand. Whether 'world-views' are considered as being in the actors' heads or analytical constructions does not change the fact that traditional behaviour cannot be described in terms of 'worlds-views', as I will try to show below.

3 This is a very brief summary of Horton's views, which cannot be discussed at length in the space of this chapter. See Boyer (1987) for a more detailed examination and criticism.

4 Advocates of the 'neo-intellectualist' approach would of course argue that this is not a definitive argument against the existence of traditional 'theories'. What we need here is just a 'looser' concept of theory, for which the requirements of explicitness and consistency are not so rigid. This, however, will not do, because it means trivialising the meaning of the word 'theory' to such an extent that 'having a theory' about something is nothing more than having 'some ideas' or 'thoughts' about it. In any case, there are more important arguments against the neo-intellectualist view of tradition, namely that it is based on an imaginary version of human cognition, and that it makes most traditional phenomena totally puzzling. I will return to this question in the following chapters. If we consider traditions as the expression of theories, then it is impossible to understand why some traditional categories cannot be defined, why rituals make constant use of obscure speech-forms, why divination is convincing. In other words, the theory is neither psychologically plausible nor anthropologically explanatory; this I suppose is enough to justify the search for an alternative.

5 The following section is a very sketchy description of the complex network of representations and beliefs about Fang epic poetry. Boyer (1981, 1982) gives a more detailed account and some information about the ethnographic background.

6 This, obviously, is only a very brief summary of the argument, which is developed

121.

at length in Boyer 1988, especially about recent changes, between Zwè Nguéma in the 1950s and mvet singing in the 1980s. Tessmann (1913) is a very detailed ethnographic study of all aspects of Fang culture, which gives some indications about the importance of clan warfare at the time.

7 The analogy is pervasive in anthropology, and the preservation and modification of cultural traits is often seen as a cultural 'selection' of ideas, formally analogous to the selection of individuals in Darwinism. On this, and the ambiguities of this common idea, see Ingold 1986. I will return to this analogy in the section dealing with automatic versus intentional repetition, see pp. 13–20.

8 All these problems, to do with the inference of notions from specific statements and actions, are examined in great detail by Holy and Stuchlik (1983: 55–80), whose general outlook is more optimistic than mine, as they suggest that the problems are mainly methodological. Also, Holy and Stuchlik do not seem to consider the difference between representing an event and representing a general description. For instance, they assume that 'all actions are guided by relevant knowledge' (1983: 68) and presuppose that such knowledge consists in general rules and models. They therefore do not consider the possibility, which I will explore in the following chapters, that the 'relevant knowledge' in question consists of memories of previous actions, with no 'theoretical' principles to organise them.

9 An additional argument for this is that some aspects of interaction are repeated without being represented at all by the actors. People cannot be conservative about what they do not represent. This point will be examined below, in the discussion of non-intentional models of repetition.

10 This commonsense view of human memory as a bucket filled with pictures and words is now reinforced by computer analogies. What are called 'memories' in computers *do* consist of devices which just store what they are fed and feed it back in the same form. Needless to say, this is a very bad metaphor for human memory, which is a processing and integrating device as much as a storing mechanism.

11 There is a third alternative, that of a Durkheimian 'collective memory' (see Halbwachs 1925, and Douglas 1982). Although the conceptual frameworks are entirely different, the ideas put forward in this section are consistent with at least one of Halbwachs points, namely that social interaction need not be totally represented to be reproduced. The idea of 'collective memory', however, entails a 'superorganic' view of culture which is precisely what I am trying to avoid in the characterisation of tradition.

12 Some psychological conditions of memory for stories were first described in Bartlett's famous studies (1932: see also Bartlett 1923 and 1958 for the general framework). The hypotheses presented here are often inspired by Bartlett's results and speculative claims. For a more recent and detailed study of structural constraints on stories (and a survey of the literature) see Beaugrande 1982.

How to think with 'empty' notions

1 I will not discuss here the Wittgensteinian or 'linguistic philosophy' idea that conceptual analysis is quite sufficient, and that in fact it is all there is to do in order to describe theories and conceptions. Although such ideas once had some influence in anthropology (see Gellner 1974, 1979 for a survey and criticism), the psychological implications are just too implausible to deserve a lengthy discussion. The rest of this chapter in fact provides some arguments against such inferences from linguistic use to theoretical premises.

2 The following is a very brief description of the ideas associated with evur. A detailed description of the rituals concerned with evur-related diseases, and a general *exposé* of the system, can be found in Mallart-Guimera 1975, 1981. A more limited description, to do with evur and epic singing, can be found in Boyer 1988. On the notion itself and the general anthropological problem, see Boyer 1986, 1989a.

3 For other examples of such notions, see the essays gathered in Fogelson and Adams (ed., 1977), although the hypotheses presented in this collection are not entirely satisfactory. Most of the contributors think that the notions in questions are concepts of 'power' and take this gloss as an unproblematic translation. Also, they all consider that the analysis should focus on the 'cultural theories' about such concepts, a claim which I discuss in the following pages.

4 Keesing's paper is also important in the sense that it shows how anthropology has a built-in tendency to see 'cultural metaphysics' in local categories, which in some cases are used as simple conventional metaphors. I will return to this point in chapter 3 (see pp. 48ff, and note 4). Keesing 1985 gives a more detailed criticism of 'anthropological metaphysics' and expands on the notion of conventional metaphors. For a discussion of the relevance of this concept, see Boyer 1989a.

5 This of course is a simplified version of a rather complicated text, the formulation of which makes the discussion difficult.

6 This criticism applies to many anthropological constructions, besides the structuralist idea that traditional categories can be construed as 'empty signifiers'. The idea that language embodies or carried cultural 'theories' is pervasive in anthropology, and the argument of this chapter is precisely to show how this assumption precludes an empirical study of the way categories are actually used.

7 This is the only way of making plausible that Fang people have 'theories' about evur. But the claim then is trivial. No-one would deny that Fang people have thoughts about evur, or that such thoughts are organised to some extent. But then there is no form of thinking or cognitive activity that is not 'theoretical' in that sense, so that the term is useless, as I mentioned above (see chapter 1, note 4).

8 The question of the type of 'knowledge' transmitted in initiation rites, and of the other cognitive effects of initiation, is discussed in more detail in the first sections of chapter 6.

9 For the sake of argument, I admit here that some concepts may be represented with a mental definition. If on the other hand we accept, like many linguists and most psychologists, that virtually no terms can be defined and that the resources of the common vocabulary are more or less equivalent to conceptual resources, then this holds *a fortiori* for traditional categories. On the idea that definitions are not 'psychologically real', see J. D. Fodor *et al.* (1975), J. A. Fodor *et al.* (1980).

10 On the notion of natural kinds, a basic reference is Schwarz (1979), with a simple distinction between 'natural' and 'nominal' kinds. See also Churchland (1985), and Schwarz (ed., 1977), for various contributions on natural kinds and linguistic reference. The representation of natural kinds and the parallel with some traditional categories are discussed again in the second part of chapter 6, about traditional positions (p. 101ff). See also Boyer 1989a for a general discussion of pseudo-natural kinds in traditional interactions.

11 A classical source on the various theories of concept representation is Smith and Medin (1981). The view of natural kinds presented here is clearly inspired by Putnam's account (1975, 1983). However, the claims made here are neutral as concerns controversies on the format of conceptual representations. Whatever the exact format of stereotypes, they are *not* what one acquires through initiation rites or other traditional situations.

12 Obviously, the problem is to describe the mechanism whereby people pick out certain common features of exemplars and discard others in the construction of a stereotype. For general surveys of theories and arguments about this abstraction process, see Posner and Keele (1968), Carey (1978, 1982, 1985) and MacNamara (1982).

13 This hypothesis is defended in Boyer (1986), where 'evur' and such terms as 'mana', 'mangu', 'orenda', etc., are construed as essentially similar. This however is refuted, partly by empirical arguments (see Keesing 1984, for instance, for a better analysis of 'mana', and Boyer 1989a for comments), and partly for theoretical reasons explained in the following pages. The interesting aspect of traditional notions concerns the process whereby they are anchored to specific experiences, and this can apply to virtually any kind of concepts.

14 The ancestor-cults, in which the notion of bekong is crucial, are described in detail in Fernandez (1982). See also Mallart-Guimera (1981) for the connections between evur and bekong.

15 See Tulving (1983 *passim*) for a presentation of the distinction and the case for the existence of separate mechanisms. The reasons why some psychologists are reluctant are (i) the fact that certain memorised elements, like e.g. scripted actions, seem neither 'episodic' nor 'semantic' in essence, and (ii) the fact that it may be wrong to infer, from different types of memorised material (episodes vs. general propositions) to different devices (see Anderson and Ross 1980). The argument developed here only implies that episodic material exists and is processed as such, a fact that no psychologist seems to deny, yet is obviously ignored in anthropological theories.

Criteria of truth

1 See Luther (1935) and Detienne (1966) for symmetrical, perhaps complementary interpretations of the evolution of *aletheia* in Archaic times. While Luther seeks to describe the evolution from mythical to philosophical conceptions of truth, Detienne treats *aletheia* as a term of the vocabulary, the usage of which can be described in terms of oppositions and implications. My argument on truth-terms is partly inspired by Detienne's stimulating account, although he does not base his argument on the idea that logical truth predicates are always present, whatever the metaphorical terms which denote them.

2 Obviously, Gutmann's argument, like all arguments from etymology, is dubious in that it presupposes that people's use of a term is influenced by the term's derivation. But not all arguments on 'specific concepts of truth', different from logical concepts, are based on such etymological inferences, so I will not discuss this specific flaw.

3 This of course is a postulate. The Aristotelian characterisation is the simplest and the clearest one available. Also, it has the advantage of highlighting the 'redundancy' of truth-ascriptions, a point to which I will return presently.

4 Keesing (1984, 1985) gives a clear exposition of Lakoff's argument and its anthropological implications, especially against 'anthropological metaphysics', a point I mentioned in chapter 2 (see p. 29ff.).

5 Obviously, there are many more arguments against the idea that some people do not possess the truth predicates in their conceptual equipment. For instance, it would be difficult for small children to play (e.g., to pretend they are mice and dragons) if they did not have a concept that includes the logical predicates of truth and falsity. Also, they would have difficulties learning to lie. More generally,

truth-terms in all languages pass the test of redundancy which is typical of truth predicates. If I say that "'snow is white' is abele", this sentence too is abele. Only truth-predicates can have this effect, which is the basis of redundancy accounts of truth predicates; asserting that a sentence is true has the same value as asserting the sentence itself (see, e.g., Strawson 1949).

6 The existence of 'covert categories' (i.e., unnamed concepts in folk taxonomies) is a salient example of the complex relationships between vocabulary and mental concepts. An even simpler illustration is given by the existence of ontological categories (about what types of things there are in the world) which are not named. In Keil's experiments for instance (1979, 1986), children make inferences about new terms on the assumption that they design living things rather than artefacts, although their vocabulary does not include terms like 'living' or 'artefact'.

7 The idea of explaining strange traditional truths by resorting to specific modalities of belief is in fact so entrenched that it seems to resist even the most clearly and carefully argued exposition of the ambiguities and problems generated by the very notion of 'belief'. Needham (1972) is a good example of such an argument; although its results should be devastating for most theories based on the notion of belief, it is simply ignored. I will make another attempt here (a side attack, as it were) to show that the notion, even if it was clear, would be useless.

Customised speech (I): truth without intentions

1 For instance, the English *Poor Robin*, a seventeenth-century parody of the then popular astrological almanacs, includes the following prediction: 'we may expect some showers or rain either this month or the next, or the next after that, or else we shall have a very dry spring' (quoted by Thomas, 1971: 398).

2 This is all the more surprising, as many anthropological arguments about divination were put forward in the context of abstract discussions about the 'rationality' of divination procedures. As a result, they tended to emphasise the cognitive dimensions of divination as opposed to its practical purposes. This of course is only part of the story. Many divinatory statements concern current, not future states of affairs; they relate them to non-observable entities, e.g., gods or ancestors, instead of making claims about their subsequent evolution. Moreover, divination is often more directed to decision-making than to understanding the world, so that 'prediction' is replaced with directives.

3 This description is of course truncated, since people's representations of the actual problem at hand (e.g., bad crops or disease) are left aside. The reason for not mentioning them here is that I am trying to describe what is *specific* to the divinatory diagnosis, as opposed to other statements that could be made on the current problem. I will therefore focus on these elements (the procedure and the link established between undefined 'situation' and 'diagnosis') which would not be present in other types of statements.

4 Cicero himself makes an analogous distinction, in Quintus's plea for divination (*De Div.* I.vi.12), between 'natural' and 'artificial', and then between different types of artificial divination. The 'natural' type belongs to what anthropologists would rather call 'inductive' divination, i.e., the observation of natural portents - (clouds, etc.) and the extension of these principles to other domains.

5 The *directly* intentional interpretation (following which the oracle is a direct message from the god) was of course disputed, but only because it seemed to imply that the god was at the client's disposal. Plutarch for instance is quite

definite that it is unreasonable to say that the god himself has composed the poem; it is therefore unreasonable to find the oracles less reliable when they are expressed in prose. The god only gives the 'original stimulation' (*Pyth. Orac.* 397c). An alternative hypothesis was that the oracles were triggered, not by the god but by less worthy 'daemons', a solution which made it possible to salvage the god's transcendence, while maintaining the idea of divination as communication.

6 There is another reason for the apparent plausibility of the semiotic interpretation, which is specific to Western culture. Ever since the Renaissance, theories about 'correspondences' and 'signatures' have been diffused and influential. The idea that there are hidden connections in natural phenomena, and that some links of resemblance connect objects from different realms, was a major tenet of the Renaissance return to Platonism, and I think the influence of that model may still be at work in some anthropological models. The idea of signatures, which is most strongly argued by such influential authors as Paracelsus, was subsequently discarded by scientific inquiry. Precisely for that reason, however, I suppose it remains the model Westerners spontaneously build, when dealing with 'occult' knowledge and activities; it may also be the model people engaged in such activities, even nowadays, try to follow.

7 For a good illustration of this, see Humphrey's study of Buryat omens (1976). The Buryat single out many natural events as ominous. Although some recurrent features may be found in the events thus highlighted, there is no systematic correspondence between omen and explanation. Rather, explanations are 'free-floating', as Humphrey puts it, so that they are selected by virtue of their relevance to the problem at hand.

8 This of course is extremely short, and cannot be substantiated in the space of this chapter, which is more focused on divination in the usual, 'instrumental' or 'inspired' sense than on natural portents.

9 See Boyer (1989b) for more details on common anthropological ways of explaining strange causal inferences.

10 Here I am only giving the conclusions of arguments explained elsewhere (Boyer 1989b), and I cannot but give a few references to substantiate the main point. The inability of philosophical analyses of 'cause' to explain everyday causal judgements is illustrated in Hart and Honore's famous study on *Causation in the Law* (1959). A classical source for conceptions of causality is Mackie (1974). As for cognitive research on causal inferences, see Laurendau and Pinard (1962) for a classical Piagetian framework and Carey (1985) for its refutation. Perception of core cases of causal connection by infants is explored in Leslie (1979) and the role of background knowledge is examined in Schustack and Sternberg (1981) among others.

11 The 'photograph analogy' is often used in theories of linguistic reference, especially in 'historical' theories, following which a term like 'giraffe' refers to giraffes if there is a historical (causal) connection between the use of the term and actual tokens of the species 'giraffe'. See Evans (1982: 76–9 and 81ff.) for a survey of these theories and the ambiguity of the photograph model. Needless to say, I am not attributing this theory to diviners and their clients. The hypothesis put forward about divination only implies that people consider certain singular speech events as caused by certain singular situations. Such assumptions precisely do *not* constitute a 'theory' of truth or reference, they provide specific criteria of truth.

12 This distinction is explained in more detail in chapter 5, in the examination of iconicity in ritual languages.

Customised speech (II): truth without meaning

1 For a general description of 'special languages', see Halliday 1976. Although secret codes and languages are extremely common, there is no extensive study of their form and usage. About the use of secret codes in initiation rites, see Boyer 1980, especially about the relationship between the choice of certain formal procedures in the creation of the code on the one hand, and the status of the groups concerned on the other.

2 Sherzer is quite definite on the fact that the ordinary language translations are seen as useful helps for non-specialists, which however do not carry the same guarantees of truth as the original. On this and other aspects of the specialised discourse, see Severi 1985, and forthcoming.

3 Obviously, this is a recurrent problem in anthropological theories which focus on the 'conceptions' allegedly expressed in traditional contexts. In the study of oral literature, for instance, one is often faced with the same dilemma. If we analyse stories in terms of underlying cultural 'theories', we focus on aspects which, if they are there at all, cannot be relevant for the listeners. So it becomes difficult to explain why the stories are actually told and memorised. If, on the other hand, we want to explain this, then we must focus on the mechanisms whereby the stories communicate new ideas or reorganise old ones, in other words, on what is *not* prior common knowledge. On this precise point, see Boyer 1982a, 1984, 1987.

4 For a clear exposition of information in 'information theory' (and of the possible misinterpretations), see Dretske 1981, which also deals with the relationship between 'information' in this narrow sense, on the one hand, and linguistic meaning, on the other.

5 Obviously, Bloch's is an 'asymptotic' argument. In actual fact, formalisation only *tends* to eliminate choice, and therefore *tends* to force listeners into the dilemma of either accepting the whole discourse or else dissenting. In the discussion I will take this into account, and the arguments are supposed to show that even as a hypothesis about 'tendencies', it is insufficient.

6 See the beginning of chapter 4. The obsessive emphasis on the fact that diviners can 'manipulate' their statements implies that the procedure is, to some extent, an obstacle to the expert's insightful diagnoses.

7 Although I only discuss Bloch's hypotheses, they are representative of an anthropological tendency to interpret 'efficient' speech and all ritualised speech forms in terms of speech acts. The idea of applying speech acts models to magical utterances (spells, for instance) was first put forward by Tambiah (1968) and Finnegan (1969). The main idea is that people who recite magical incantations are not making claims about a causal connection between the words and the subsequent effects. They are in fact making a special speech-act, comparable to wishing, swearing, cursing, etc. Ahern (1979, 1982) is an example of such a speech act explanation of magical action. Gardner (1983) presents a general criticism of these attempts, which rely on a rather distorted view of the intellectual mechanisms involved, and only account for marginal aspects of the rituals. In chapter 5, I present a picture of causal thinking which I think makes it possible to understand that magical claims are causal claims, without necessarily implying a strange conception of causation.

The criticisms against Bloch's formulation of course apply also to Finnegan and Tambiah, who seem to take the phrase 'illocutionary force' literally, as denoting some form of energy. I have chosen to insist on Bloch's formulation because it is subtler, and also because Bloch tries to give some explanation of the idea that more formalisation seems to result in more efficacy, while the other authors take that as almost self-evident.

8 The clearest account of 'illocutionary force' in various pragmatic theories can be found in Levinson (1983). On the question of the relationship between propositional structure and illocution, see Katz 1977.

9 To be fair, Bloch's formulation suggests that there is a distinction between illocutionary and perlocutionary aspects of discourse. But the main hypothesis is that, in ritual speech at least, the illocutionary force of certain utterances is such that certain effects (notably persuasion) are inevitable. In short, certain typical perlocutionary effects are directly determined by illocutionary properties. This is where Bloch's account is consonant with the magic-as-speech-acts school mentioned above (see this chapter, note 7), which claims that the alleged 'effects' of spells are a simple consequence of their illocutionary properties.

10 For other examples of such phenomena, see, e.g., Jakobson's remarks on Russian parallelism and glossolalia (1966, 1981). The hypothesis on iconicity presented here is of course inspired by Jakobson's ideas, although his notion of 'poetic function' does not have much explanatory power as concerns the cognitive effects of such manipulations of language. See Kiparsky (1976) for a treatment of idioms, formulaic speech and, more generally, 'fixed' expressions in the context of generative-transformational grammars.

11 What I have presented here is a very abstract description; an empirical investigation should describe more precisely in what manner the existence of causal criteria of truth results in the repetition of traditional events. I will return to this crucial point in chapter 7.

Customised persons: initiation, competence and position

1 I am aware of the vagueness of this general characterisation, although I would claim that these features are really general, and the necessary starting point of a theory of initiations. A more detailed account, which is more or less compatible with what I say in the following sections, can be found in J. La Fontaine's general survey (1985). For the sake of clarity I only consider the case of collective ('tribal') initiations, although what I say about them applies, *mutatis mutandis*, to personal initiations as well. See Boyer 1980, 1984 for the analysis of both types of institutions.

2 There is no space here to comment on the cognitive effects of such deceptive 'revelations'. A typical, yet paradoxical effect is that they seem to reinforce the neophytes' conviction that the rite is indeed important, that there is more than meets the eye in ritual procedures, which cannot be reduced to the farcical staging. The mechanisms of this effect are not entirely clear, though. See Barth 1975 for a detailed exposition, Boyer 1980 and Houseman 1984 for a discussion.

3 This of course is directly related to the fact that ritual idioms, though they are supposed to convey important truths, have very little 'propositional potential'; see the discussion in chapter 5.

4 Herdt's collection on male initiation in Papua New Guinea (1982) gives a good survey of particularly paradoxical forms of initiation, in which 'knowledge' and painful ordeals are intimately connected. The essays in this volume also focus on the emotive aspects of the ordeals, which are obviously crucial.

5 For a characterisation of positions in terms of rights and duties, see for instance Bendix and Lipset (1966), or Goodenough's 'componential' analysis of statuses and roles (1965). Positions in that framework are abstract combinations, which are not necessarily represented by the actors. Goodenough makes a clear distinction

between objective statuses and represented 'social categories'. Only the latter is the subject matter of my argument.

6 I am not denying here that the distribution of positions can be said to constitute a system. But this idea often relies on the assumption that positions are mentally defined, which I think is not true in the case of the positions implied in traditional interaction.

7 There is an extensive literature on these low-status endogamous groups and the symbolic justification of their exclusion. See Tuden and Plotnicov's collection (1970) for a general survey, especially Vaughan's essay. Whether such groups can be called 'castes' or not is of course a terminological more than a substantial question (Todd 1977). They have all the features associated with castes in the usual, non- or pre-Dumont use of the term (Berreman 1968). One can apply to such groups the general claims made by Hocart about the connection between position and social categorising; this is argued in Boyer (1982b).

8 These stories are compared and analysed in Boyer (1982b), with a contrast with non-endogamous, high-status blacksmith lineages in Central Africa.

9 This of course is a drastically shortened version of the processes involved in the representation of natural kinds, especially living kinds. See the references in chapter 2, note 10.

10 See also Keil 1986. These experiments, and their anthropological consequences, are discussed in Boyer 1989a, where it is argued that most complex cultural categories are linked to the identification of 'pseudo-kinds'. The notions therefore carry no 'theory' of the entities designated, only the presumption that such entities share essential properties in the same way as living kinds. The connection, between representing 'mystical' entities as members of living kinds, and ascribing to them specific causal features, is discussed in Boyer 1989b.

11 The claim here concerns only what I called 'traditional' positions, i.e., positions the identification of which is required in traditional interaction, although it is probable that such cognitive mechanisms apply to other domains of social categorisation.

Conclusions and programme

1 This is necessarily a very brief presentation; Chafe's and Goody's hypotheses are in fact much more refined. The psychological differences studied by Hildyard and Olson (1982) concern both understanding and memorisation. Oral communication allows better recall, and written communication better recognition of a single text. 'The listeners pay primary attention to the theme of the story, building a coherent representation of what was meant. The readers, on the other hand, are able to pay closer attention to the meaning of the sentences *per se*, recalling more incidental explicit details' (Hildyard and Olson 1982: 31).

2 For certain limited tasks like palace bookkeeping, pictographic or ideographic systems seem much more economical than phonetic scripts. When the only use of literacy is to count measures of corn and oil in stores, using pictograms is more rational than transcribing the words 'oil' or 'corn' and the words for numbers. This is probably the simplest explanation of the persistence of pictographic elements and 'rebus' interpretations in phonetic scripts, and of the coexistence of both types of scripts, like in Mycenean civilisation, with a pictograph and a syllabary used together.

3 This of course is entirely different from the question of 'written traditions', which is outside the scope of this volume. One must notice that the introduction of writing in oral traditions does not create 'written traditions' out of them.

4 Obviously, this extension of written rational argumentation does not preclude, as the Greek case shows eloquently, the development of mystic cults and irrational sects.

5 The notion of 'claims to truth' (and of competing claims) is inspired by Lloyd 1979.

6 Varying degrees of commitment are often described in probabilistic terms, as a full belief in the fact that the considered proposition has a probability $1/x$ of being true. The application of such ideas, and of refined 'Bayesian' computations, to real inference processes is not altogether easy, however: see for instance Miller (1987: 297–347) for a discussion from a philosophical viewpoint.

7 The distinction between 'central processes' (such as attention or memorisation) and 'modular processes' (specialised in perceptual information, language parsing, etc.) was introduced by Fodor (1983), together with the idea that, while cognitive psychology is increasingly successful at describing modular functioning, it has very little hope of ever explaining how central processes work.

8 It is not possible here to examine to what extent naturalistic data are an obstacle to precise and testable arguments. Hutchins's study of land-tenure litigation in Trobriand (1980) is a vivid counter-example, which shows that a successful cognitive formalisation can be based on classical fieldwork data. Hutchins himself discusses the problem in his conclusion (1980: 125–28).

Bibliography

Adler, A. and A. Zempleni, 1972. *Le Bâton de l'Aveugle*, Paris: Editions Hermann.
Agar, M., 1974. Talking about doing. Lexicon and event, *Language and Society*, 3: 83–89.
Ahern, E. M., 1979. The problem of efficacy. Strong and weak illocutionary acts, *Man* (n.s.), 14: 1–17.
1982. Rules in oracles and games, *Man* (n.s.), 17: 302–12.
Anderson, J. R. and B. H. Ross, 1980. Evidence against a semantic/episodic distinction, *Journal of Experimental Psychology* (*Human Learning and Memory*), 6: 441–65.
Anglin, J. M., 1970. *The Growth of Word-meaning*, Cambridge: The MIT Press.
1977. *Word, Object and Conceptual Development*, New York: Norton.
Aquili, E. G., C. D. Laughlin and J. McManus, 1979. *The Spectrum of Ritual. A Biogenetic Structural Analysis*, New York: Columbia University Press.
Atran, S., 1987. Ordinary constraints on the semantics of living kinds. A commonsense alternative to recent treatments of natural-object terms, *Mind and Language* 2: 27–63.
Austin, J. L., 1962. *How To Do Things With Words*, Oxford: Clarendon Press.
Barnes, J. A., 1967. *Politics In A Changing Society*, Manchester: Manchester University Press.
Barth, F., 1975. *Ritual and Knowledge Among The Bakataman Of New Guinea*, Newhaven/Oslo: Yale University Press/Universitet-forlaget.
Bartlett, F. C., 1923. *Psychology And Primitive Culture*, Cambridge: Cambridge University Press.
1932. *Remembering. A Study In Experimental And Social Psychology*, Cambridge: Cambridge University Press.
1958. *Thinking. An Experimental And Social Study*. New York: Basic Books.
Bauer, D. F. and J. Hinnant, 1980. Normal and revolutionary divination. A Kuhnian approach to African traditional thought, in I. Karp and C. S. Bird (eds.), *Explorations In African Systems Of Thought*, Bloomington: Indiana University Press.
Beaugrande, R. de, 1982. Story of grammar and grammar of stories, *Journal of Pragmatics*, 6: 383–422.
Bellman, B. L., 1984. *The Language Of Secrecy. Symbols And Metaphors In Poro Ritual*, New Brunswick: Rutgers University Press.
Bendix, R. and R. Lipset, 1966. *Class, Status and Power. Social Stratification in Comparative Perspective*, New York: The Free Press.
Berlin, B., D. Breedlove and P. Raven, 1973. General principles of classification and nomenclature in folk-biology, *American Anthropologist*, 75: 214–42.

131

Bibliography

Berreman, G. D., 1968. The concept of 'caste', *International Encyclopaedia of the Social Sciences*, New York: McMillan and The Free Press.
Bloch, M., 1974. Symbols, song, dance and features of articulation. Is religion an extreme form of traditional authority?, *European Journal of Sociology*, 15: 55–81.
  1985. From cognition to ideology, in R. Fardon (ed.),*Power and Knowledge. Anthropological and Sociological Approaches*, Edinburgh: Scottish Academic Press.
Bohannan, L., 1952. A genealogical charter, *Africa*, 22: 301–15.
Bottero, J., 1987. *Mesopotamie*, Paris: Editions Gallimard.
Bowerman, M., 1978. The acquisition of word-meaning: an investigation into some current conflicts, in N. Waterson and C. Snow (eds.), *The Development of Communication*, New York: Wiley.
  1982. Reorganizational processes in lexical and syntactic development, in E. Wanner and L. R. Gleitman (eds.), *Language Acquisition: The State of the Art*, Cambridge: Cambridge University Press.
Boyer, P., 1980. Les Figures du savoir initiatique, *Journal des Africanistes*, 50: 31–57.
  1982a. Recit epique et tradition, *L'Homme, Revue Française d'Anthropologie*, 27: 5–34.
  1982b. Le Status des forgerons et ses justifications symboliques, *Africa*, 53: 44–63.
  1984. La Tradition comme genre enonciatif, *Poetique*, 58: 55–72.
  1986. The 'empty' concepts of traditional thinking. A semantic and pragmatic description, *Man* (n.s.), 21: 50–64.
  1987. The stuff 'traditions' are made of. On the implicit ontology of an ethnographic category,*Philosophy of the Social Sciences*, 17: 49–65.
  1988. *Barricades mystérieuses et pièges a pensée*, Paris: Société d'Ethnologie.
  1989a. Pseudo-kinds and Complex Cultural Categories, unpubl. ms.
  1989b. Causal Thinking and Its Anthropological Misrepresentation, unpubl. ms.
Boyd, R., 1980. Materialism without reductionism. What physicalism does not entail, in N. Block (ed.), *Redings in the Philosophy of Psychology*, Cambridge: The MIT Press.
Brand, M., 1976. Introduction: defining 'causes', in M. Brand (ed.), *The Nature of Causation*, Chicago: University of Illinois Press.
Carey, S., 1978. The child as word learner, in M. Halle and G. A. Miller (eds.), *Linguistic Theory And Psychological Reality*, Cambridge: The MIT Press.
  1982. Semantic development: the state of the art, in E. Wanner and L. R. Gleitman (eds.), *Language Acquisition: The State of the Art*, Cambridge: Cambridge University Press.
  1985. *Conceptual Change in Childhood*, Cambridge: The MIT Press.
Carnap, R., 1956. The methodological character of theoretical concepts, in H. Feigl and M. Scriven (eds.), *Minnesota Studies in the Philosophy of Science (I)*, Minneapolis: University of Minnesota Press.
Chafe, W., 1982. Integration and involvement in speaking, writing and oral literature, in D. Tannen (ed.), *Spoken and Written Language*, Norwood: Ablex.
Churchland, P. M., 1985. Conceptual progress and word/world relations. In search of natural kinds, *Canadian Journal of Philosophy*, 15: 1–17.
Cicourel, A., 1972. Basic and normative rules in the negociation of status and role, in D. Sudnow (ed.), *Studies in Social Interaction*, New York: The Free Press.
Clark, E. V., 1973. Non-linguistic strategies and the acquisition of word-meaning, *Cognition*, 2: 161–82.
Clement, P., 1948. Le Forgeron en Afrique Noire. Quelques attitudes du groupe a son egard, *Revue de Geographie Humanie et d'Ethnographie*, 2: 1–15.

Bibliography

Cole, M. and S. Scribner, 1974. *Culture And Thought. A Psychological Introduction*, New York: John Wiley and Sons.
Cole, M., *et al.*, 1971. *The Cultural Context of Learning and Thinking. An Exploration in Experimental Anthropology*, London: Methuen.
Craik, F. I. M. (ed.), 1979. *Levels Of Processing In Human Memory*, Hillsdale: Lawrence Erlbaum Associates.
Davidson, D., 1980. *Essays On Actions And Events*, Oxford: Clarendon Press.
Detienne, M., 1966. *Les Maîtres de vérité dans la Grèce archaïque*, Paris: François Maspero.
Dieterlen, G. and Y. Cissé, 1972. *Les Fondements de la Société d'Initiation du Komo*, Paris/The Hague: Mouton and Co.
Dougherty, J. D. W. (ed.), 1985. *Directions in Cognitive Anthropology*, Urbana/Chicago: University of Illinois Press.
Douglas, M., 1982. *In the Active Voice*, London: Routledge and Kegan Paul.
Dretske, F., 1981. *Knowledge and the Flow of Information*, Oxford: Basil Blackwell.
Eisenstadt, S. N., 1956. *From Generation to Generation*, London: The Free Press.
Evans, G., 1982. *The Varieties of Reference*, Oxford: Clarendon Press.
Evans-Pritchard, E. E., 1937. *Witchcraft, Oracles and Magic among the Azande*, Oxford: Clarendon Press.
Favret Saada, J., 1980. *Deadly Words*, Cambridge/Paris: Cambridge University Press/Maison des Sciences de l'Homme.
Favret Saada, J. and J. Contreras, 1984. Comment produire de l'energie avec deux jeux de cartes, *Bulletin d'Ethnomèdecine* 24.
Fernandez, J. W., 1982. *Bwiti. An Ethnography of the Religious Imagination in Africa*, Princeton: Princeton University Press.
1986. *Persuasions and Performances. The Play of Tropes in Culture*, Bloomington: Indiana Unversity Press.
Finnegan, R., 1969. How to do things with words: performative utterances among the Limba of Sierra Leone, *Man* (n.s.), 4: 57–51.
Fodor, J. A., 1981. *Representations. Philosophical Essays on the Foundations of Cognitive Science*, Cambridge: The MIT Press.
1983. *The Modularity Of Mind. An Essay On Faculty Psychology*, Cambridge: The MIT Press.
Fodor, J. A. *et al.*, 1980. Against definitions, *Cognition*, 8: 263–367.
Fodor, J. D. *et al.*, 1975. The psychological unreality of semantic representations, *Linguistic Inquiry*, 6: 515–31.
Fogelson, R. D. and R. N. Adams (eds.), 1977. *The Anthropology of Power*, New York: Academic Press.
Fortes, M., 1966. Religious premises and logical technique in divinatory ritual, *Philosophical Transactions of the Royal Society of London*, 251: 409–22.
Gardner, D. S., 1983. Performativity and ritual: the Mianmin case, *Man* (n.s.), 18: 346–60.
Gasking, D., 1955. Causation and recipes. *Mind*, 64: 479–87.
Gellner, E., 1974. *The Legitimation of Belief*, Cambridge: Cambridge University Press.
1979. *Spectacles and Predicaments. Essay in Social Theory*, Cambridge: Cambridge University Press.
Gelman, S., 1988. The development of induction within natural kind and artefact categories, *Cognitive Psychology*, 20: 65–95.
Gelman, S. and E. Markman, 1987. Young children's inductions from natural kinds: the role of categories and appearances, *Child Development*, 58: 32–41.

133

Genest, S., 1976. La Transmission du savoir chez les Forgerons Mafa *(Nord-Cameroun)*, Ph.D. Dissertation, University of Paris-Sorbonne.

Goodenough, W., 1965. Rethinking 'status' and 'role', in M. Banton (ed.), *The Relevance of Models for Social Anthropology*, London: Tavistock Publications.

Goodman, N., 1954. *Fact, Fiction and Forecast*, Cambridge: Harvard Unversity Press.

Goody, J. R., 1977. *The Domestication of the Savage Mind*, Cambridge: Cambridge University Press.

1986. *The Logic of Writing and the Organisation of Society*, Cambridge: Cambridge University Press.

1987. *The Interface of the Oral and the Written*, Cambridge: Cambridge University Press.

Goody, J. R. and I. Watt, 1968. The consequences of literacy, in J. R. Goody (ed.), *Literacy in Traditional Societies*, Cambridge: Cambridge University Press.

Gutmann, B., 1926. *Das Recht der Dschagga*, Munich.

Halbwachs, M., 1925. *Les Cadres sociaux de la memoire*, Paris: Felix Alcan.

Halliday, M. A. K., 1976. Anti-language, *American Anthropologist*, 78: 570–84.

Hallpike, C. R., 1979. *The Foundations of Primitive Thought*, Oxford: Clarendon Press.

Hart, H. L. A. and T. Honoré, 1959. *Causation in the Law*, Oxford: Clarendon Press.

Herdt, G. (ed.) 1982. *Rituals of Manhood. Male Initiation in Papua New Guinea*, Berkeley: University of California Press.

Hildyard, A. and T. R. Olson, 1982. On the comprehension and memory of oral vs. written discourse, in D. Tannen (ed.), *Spoken and Written Language. Exploring Orality and Literacy*, Norwood: Ablex.

Hirschfeld, L. A., 1988. On acquiring social knowledge, *Man*, 23.

Hollis, M., 1970. Reason and ritual, in B. Wilson (ed.), *Rationality*, Oxford: Basil Blackwell.

Hollis, M., and S. Lukes (eds.), 1982. *Rationality and Relativism*, Oxford: Basil Blackwell.

Holy, L. and M. Stuchlik, 1983. *Actions, Norms and representations. Foundations of Anthropological Inquiry*, Cambridge: Cambridge University Press.

Horton, R., 1967a, b. African traditional thought and modern science, *Africa*, 38: 50–71 and 155–87.

1970. African traditional thought and modern science, in B. Wilson (ed.), *Rationality*, Oxford: Basil Blackwell.

1982. Tradition and modernity revisited, in M. Hollis and S. Lukes (eds.), *Rationality and Relativism*, Oxford: Basil Blackwell.

Houseman, M., 1984. Les Artifices de la logique initiatique, *Journal des Africanistes*, 54: 41–65.

1986. Le Mal pour le Mâle, un bien initiatique, in J. Hainard and R. Kaehr (eds.), *Le Mal et la douleur*, Neuchatel: Institut d'Ethnologie.

Humphrey, C., 1976. Omens and their explanation among the Buryat, *European Journal of Sociology*, 17: 21–38.

Hutchins, E., 1980. *Culture and Inference. A Trobriand Case Study*, Cambridge: Harvard University Press.

1981. Reasoning in Trobriand discourse, in R. W. Casson (ed.), *Language, Culture and Cognition*, New York: Macmillan.

Hymes, D., 1974. Ways of speaking, in R. Bauman and J. Sherzer (eds.), *Explorations in the Ethnography of Speaking*, Cambridge: Cambridge University Press.

Ingold, T., 1986. *Evolution and Social Life*, Cambridge: Cambridge University Press.

Jakobson, R., 1966. Retrospect, in R. Jakobson, *Selected Writings IV: Early Slavic Paths and Crossroads*, The Hague/New York: Mouton.

1981. Grammatical parallelism and its Russian facet, in R. Jakobson, *Selected Writings III: Poetry of Grammar and Grammar of Poetry*, The Hague/New York: Mouton.

Katz, B., G. Baker and J. MacNamara, 1974. What's in a name? On the child's acquisition of proper and common nouns, *Child Development*, 45: 269–73.

Katz, J. J., 1977. *Propositional Structure and Illocutionary Force*, New York: Thomas Y. Crowell.

Keesing, R., 1984. Rethinking Mana, *Journal of Anthropological Research*, 40: 137–56.

1985. Conventional metaphors and anthropological metaphysics: the problematic of cultural translations, *Journal of Anthropological Research*, 41: 201–17.

Keil, F. C., 1979. *Semantic and Conceptual Devlopment*, Cambridge: Harvard University Press.

1986. The acquisition of natural kind and artefact terms, in A. Marrar and W. Demopoulos (eds.), *Conceptual Change*, Norwood: Ablex.

Kiparsky, P., 1976. Oral poetry: some linguistic and typological considerations, in B. A. Stolz and R. S. Shannon (eds.), *Oral Literature and the Formula*, Ann Arbor: Michigan University Press.

La Fontaine, J. S., 1977. The power of rights, *Man* (n.s.), 12: 421–37.

1985. *Initiation. Ritual Drama and Secret Knowledge Across the World*, Harmondsworth: Penguin Books.

Lakoff, G. and M. Johnson, 1977. *Metaphors We Live By*, Chicago: University of Chicago Press.

Lakoff, G. and Z. Kovecses, 1986. The cognitive model of anger inherent in English, in D. Holland and N. Quinn (eds.), *Cultural Models in Language and Thought*, New York: Cambridge University Press.

Laurendau, M. and A. Pinard, 1962. *Causal Thinking in the Child*, New York: International Universities Press.

Lee, D. D., 1949. Being and value in a primitive culture, *Journal of Philosophy*, 8 (13): 401–15.

Leslie, A., 1979. The Representation of Perceived Causal Connection, D.Phil. thesis, University of Oxford.

Levinson, S., 1983. *Pragmatics*, Cambridge: Cambridge University Press.

Levi-Strauss, C., 1987. *Introduction to the Work of Marcel Mauss*, London: Routledge and Kegan Paul.

Lewis, G. A., 1980. *Day of Shining Red. An Essay on Understanding Ritual*, Cambridge: Cambridge University Press.

Lloyd, G. E. R., 1979. *Magic, Reason and Experience*, Cambridge: Cambridge University Press.

Loewe, M. and C. Blacker (eds.), 1981. *Divination and Oracles*, London: George Allen and Unwin.

Luhrmann, T., 1986. Witchcraft, morality and magic in contemporary London, *International Journal of Moral and Social Sciences*, I: 77–94.

Luria, A., 1976. *Cognitive Development. Its Cultural and Social Foundations*, Cambridge: Harvard University Press.

Luther, W., 1935. 'Wahrheit' und 'Liige' im ältesten Griechentum, Göttingen: Georg August Universität (Inaugural-Dissertation).

MacCulloch, J. A., 1912. Heart, in J. Hastings (ed.), *Encyclopaedia of Religion and Ethics*, Edinburgh: T. and T. Clark.

Mackie, J. L., 1974. *The Cement of the Universe*, Oxford: Clarendon Press.

135

Bibliography

MacNamara, J., 1982. *Names for Things. A Study of Human Learning*, Cambridge: The MIT Press.
Mallart-Guimera, L., 1975. Ni dos ni ventre: magie, sorcellerie et religion evuzok, *L'Homme. Revue Française d'Anthropologie*, 15: 35–65.
1981. *Ni dos ni ventre*, Paris: Société d'Ethnographie.
Maret, P. de, 1980. Ceux qui jouent avec le feu: la place du forgeron en Afrique centrale, *Africa*, 50: 263–79.
Martin, J. Y., 1970. *Les Matakam du Nord-Cameroun. Dynamismes sociaux et problemes de modernisation*, Paris: Orstom.
Mauss, M., 1951. *Sociologie et Anthropologie*, Paris: Presses Universitaires de France.
Mendonsa, E. L., 1976. *The Politics of Divination, A Processual View of Illness and Deviation among the Sisala of Northern Ghana*, Berkeley: University of California Press, 1982.
1982. Characteristics of Sisala diviners, in A. Bharati (ed.), *The Realm of the Extra-Human, Agents and Audiences*, Paris/The Hague: Mouton and Cy.
Miller, R., 1987. *Fact and Method. Explanation, Confirmation and Reality in the Natural and the Social Sciences*, Princeton: Princeton University Press.
Needham, R., 1972. *Belief, Language and Experience*, Oxford: Basil Blackwell.
1976. Skulls and causality, *Man* (n.s.), 11: 71–88.
Nuchelmans, G., 1973. *Theories of the Proposition. Ancient and Medieval Conceptions of the Bearers of Truth and Falsity*, Amsterdam: North-Holland.
1980. *Late-Scholastic and Humanist Theories of the Proposition*, Amsterdam: North-Holland.
Osherson, D. N., 1978. Three conditions on conceptual naturalness, *Cognition*, 6: 263–89.
Park, G., 1963. Divination and its social contexts, *Journal of the Royal Anthropological Institute*, 93: 195–209.
Philsooph, H., 1972. Primitive magic and Mana, *Man* (n.s.), 6: 182–203.
Posner, M. I., and S. W. Keele, 1968. On the genesis of abstract ideas, *Journal of Experimental Psychology*, 77: 353–63.
Putman, H., 1975. *Mind, Language and Reality. Philosophical Papers (II)*, Cambridge: Cambridge University Press.
1983. *Realism and Reason. Philosophical Papers (III)*, Cambridge: Cambridge University Press.
Rappaport, R. A., 1974. The obvious aspects of ritual, *Cambridge Anthropology*, 2: 3–69.
Reynolds, B., 1963. *Magic, Divination and Witchcraft among the Barotse of Northern Ghana*, London: Chatto and Windus.
Richards, A. I., 1956. *Chisunqu, A Girl's Initiation Ceremony in Northern Rhodesia*, London: Faber.
Sales, A. de, 1986. Actes et paroles dans les rituels Chamaniques des Kham Magar, Ph.D. Dissertation, University of Paris-Nanterre.
Schustack, M. W. and R. J. Sternberg, 1981. Evaluation of evidence in causal inference, *Journal of Experimental Psychology: General*, 110: 101–20.
Schwarz, S. P. (ed.), 1977. *Naming, Necessity and Natural Kinds*, Ithaca: Cornell University Press.
1979. Natural kind terms, *Cognition*, 7: 301–15.
Scribner, S., 1975. Recall of classical syllogisms. A cross-cultural investigation of error on logical problems, in R. J. Falmagne (ed.) *Reasoning: Representation and Process*, Hillsdale: Lawrence Erlbaum Associates.
Scribner, S. and M. Cole, 1981. *The Psychology of Literacy*, Cambridge: Harvard University Press.
Severi, C., 1985. Penser par séquences, penser par territoires, *Communications*, 41: 169–90.

Forthcoming. The invisible path. Ritual representation of suffering in Cuna traditional thought, *Res. Anthropology and Aesthetics*, 14: 66–81.

Sherzer, J., 1985. *Kuna Ways of Speaking. An Ethnographic Perspective*, Austin: University of Texas Press.

Shils, E., 1981. *Tradition*, London: Faber and Faber.

Shoben, E. J., 1984. Semantic and episodic memory, in R. S. Wyer and T. K. Srull (eds.), *Handbook of Social Cognition (II)*, Hillsdale: Lawrence Erlbaum Associates.

Skorupski, J., 1976. *Symbol and Theory. A Philosophical Study of Theories of Religion in Social Anthropology*, Cambridge: Cambridge University Press.

Smith, E. E., and D. L. Medin, 1981. *Categories and Concepts*, Cambridge: Harvard University Press.

Sommers, F., 1959. The ordinary language tree, *Mind*, 68: 160–85.

Southwold, M., 1979. Religious Belief, *Man* (n.s.), 14: 628–44.

Sperber, D., 1982. Apparently irrational beliefs, in M. Hollis and S. Lukes (eds.), *Rationality and Relativism*, Oxford: Basil Blackwell.

Steiner, F. B., 1954. Chagga truth. A note on Gutmann's account of the Chagga concept of truth in 'Das Recht der Dschagga', *Africa*, 24: 364–9.

Stich, S., 1983. *From Folk Psychology to Cognitive Science. The Case Against Belief*, Cambridge: The MIT Press.

Strathern, M., 1985. Knowing power and being equivocal. Three Melanesian contexts, in R. Fardon (ed.), *Power and Knowledge, Anthropological and Sociological Approaches*, Edinburgh: Scottish Academic Press.

Strawson, P. F., 1949. Truth, *Analysis*, 9: 83–97.

Tambiah, S. J., 1968. The magical power of words, *Man* (new series), 3: 175–208.

Tannen, D., 1985. Relative focus on involvement in oral and written discourse, in D. R. Olson, N. Torrance and A. Hildyard (eds.), *Literacy, Language and Learning. The Nature and Consequences of Reading and Writing*, Cambridge: Cambridge University Press.

Taylor, R., 1963, Causation, *The Monist*, 47: 287–313.

Tessmann, G., 1913. *Die Pangwe. Völkerkundliche Monographie eines westafrikanischen Negerstammes*, Berlin: Ernst Wasmuth.

Thomas, K., 1971. *Religion and the Decline of Magic. Studies in Popular Beliefs in 16th and 17th-century England*, London: Weidenfeld and Nicolson.

Todd, D. M., 1977. Caste in Africa? *Africa*, 47 (4): 398–412.

Tuden, A. and L. Plotnicov (eds.), 1970. *Social Stratification in Africa*, New York: The Free Press.

Tulving, E., 1983. *Elements of Episodic Memory*, Oxford: Clarendon Press.

Ullmann, S., 1962. *Semantics. An Introduction to the Science of Meaning*, New York: Barnes and Noble.

Urban, W. M., 1939. *Language and Reality*, London: George Allen and Unwin.

Vaughan, J. H., 1970. Caste systems in the Western Sudan, in A. Tuden and L. Plotnicov (eds.), *Social Stratification in Africa*, New York: The Free Press.

Vendler, Z., 1967. Causal relations, *Journal of Philosophy*, 64: 704–13.

Vernant, J. P. (ed.), 1974. *Divination et rationalite*, Paris: Editions du Seuil.

Weil, E., 1971. Tradition et traditionnalisme, in E. Weil, *Essais et Conferences (I)*, Paris: Librairie Plon.

Wilson, B. (ed.), 1980. *Rationality*, Oxford: Basil Blackwell.

Zeitlyn, D., 1987. Mambila divination, *Cambridge Anthropology*, 12: 20–51.

Zempleni, A., 1986. La 'Maladie' et ses 'causes', *L'Ethnographie* (new series), 4: 1–34.

Zwè Nguéma, 1972. *Un mvet de Zwè Nguéma*, Paris: Armand Colin.

Index

138

Index

Fodor, J. D., 123, 133
Fogelson, 123, 133
force, 'vital', 26
formalised speech, 82ff.
Fortes, 66, 71, 133

Gardner, 97–8, 127, 133
Gellner, 113, 122, 133
Gelman, 104, 133
Genest, 102, 133
Gisu, 96
Goodenough, 128, 134
Goody, 114–15, 129, 134
great divide, see tradition, definitions of
Gutmann, 49, 124, 134

Halbwachs, 122, 134
Halliday, 127, 134
Hart, 126, 134
Herdt, 128, 134
Hildyard, 115, 129, 134
Hinnant, 65, 132
Hocart, 129
Hollis, 52, 56, 134
holy, 121–22, 134
Honoré, 126, 134
Horton, 4–5, 28, 121, 134
Houseman, 96, 128, 134
Humphrey, 126, 134
Hutchins, 130, 134

iconicity, 88, 128
illocutionary force, 82–83, 85–86, 128
iloha, 49
Ingold, 18, 122, 134
initiation: and causal criteria, 97ff.; and
    knowledge, 95ff., 128
interaction, representation of, 18–20

Jakobson, 128, 134

Katz, 128, 135
Keele, 124, 136
Keesing, 27, 123–24, 135
Keil, 125, 129, 135
Kham-Magar, 87
Kiparsky, 128, 135

La Fontaine, 96, 128, 135
Lakoff, 124, 135
Laurendeau, 126, 135
Leslie, 126, 135
Levi-Strauss, 27, 135
Levinson, 128, 135
Lewis, 3, 135

Lipset, 128, 131
literacy, 114–16, 129
literalism, 11–12, 17, 92–93
living kinds, see natural kind terms
Lloyd, 116, 130, 135
Loewe, 65, 135
lohi, 49
Luhrmann, 112, 135
Lukes, 52, 135
Luther, 124, 135

machin, 27–28
Mackie, 126, 135
MacNamara, 124, 135
Madagascar, 82ff., 89–90
magic, 127
Malinowski, vii
Mallart-Guimera, 35, 123–4, 136
Mambila, 71
mana, 27, 124
Maret, 101, 136
Markman, 104, 133
Martin, 102, 136
Mauss, 27, 136
Medin, 123, 137
meduk, 48ff.
memory, 16–17, 41–44, 122, 124
Mendonsa, 62, 70, 136
Merina, 82ff., 89–90
Mianmin, 97–98
Miller, 130, 136
Mundang, 70ff.
mvet, 6–8

natural kind terms, 38, 104–5, 123, 129
Navajo, vii
Needham, 76, 125, 136
neo-intellectualism, 4–5, 121
ngengang, 34ff.
Nuer, vii, 53

Olson, 115, 129, 134
ostension, 36ff.

Paracelsus, 126
perlocution, 86, 128
Pinard, 126, 135
Plotnicov, 129, 137
Plutarch, 125–26
positions: naturalised, 103–6, 109; and
    occupation, 101–5, 128, 129; and truth,
    94ff., 99–101
Posner, 124, 136
propositional potential, 82ff., 127
psychology: *ad-hoc* versions of, ix; and

Cambridge Studies in
Social Anthropology

Editor: JACK GOODY

141

*AVAILABLE IN PAPERBACK